RUINS REUSED

Changing Attitudes to Ruins
Since the Late Eighteenth Century

Pitt-Rivers in the field, drawn by Tomkin

RUINS REUSED

*Changing Attitudes to Ruins
Since the Late Eighteenth Century*

ॐ

Michael Thompson

Ruins Reused

© Michael Thompson

ISBN(10) 1-905223-04-8
ISBN(13) 978-1-905223-04-6

Cover Image: Castle Acre Priory, Norfolk, from the air. (Photo: Aerial Archaeology)

Typeset and published 2006 by:

Marketing & Publications Ltd

Hill Farm – Unit F
Castle Acre Road
Great Dunham
King's Lynn
Norfolk, PE32 2LP
Tel: 01760 755645
Fax: 01760 755316
Email: publishing@heritagemp.com
Website: www.heritagemp.com

Contents

Preface

This book is not a second edition of my book 'Ruins: their Preservation and Display' for British Museum Publications in 1981, which was a matter of nuts and bolts, methods and results; this one tries to describe the personalities and motives of the people involved with ruins in this country and the later entry of the State into the field. Towards the end of the book the purpose of preservation of ruins is discussed. It has been prompted by some of the fervent support of 'restoration' among archaeologists (not I think among architects), a matter much influenced by the supposed need of tourists, for tourists would be the main target of 'restoration'. The book may then be of interest to the general reader for he is as often as not this kind of tourist. The disappearance of the old Works organisation, in name at all events, is perhaps another good reason for looking back at it, but this subject has been treated rather more perfunctorily than it deserves. Although I had thirty years at the sharp end of preservation I now tend to write about it, rather than do it in the field.

Michael Thompson

Cambridge 2006

List of Illustrations

Acknowledgements

It is always a pleasure to record the courtesy of various bodies who have allowed the use of material in their care and helpful advice or references given by colleagues.

The Librarian of Cardiff Central Library has allowed me to quote from the transcripts of Hoare's travel diaries that I published and use Hoare's sketch in figure 4. The drawings by Tomkin in the Pitt-Rivers field notebooks in figures 1, 13 and 14, are in the National Archive (Works39/1–16). The drawings by Sir Richard Colt Hoare in figures 2, 3, 8 and 9 reproduced by permission of Llyfrgell Genedlaethol Cymru/The National Library of Wales. Figures 11, 23, 34 and 35, in Crown Copyright, are from *Cadw* at Cardiff. Figures 24 and 33 are from the Cambridge University Collection of Aerial Photographs. Burges's sections of Castell Coch, in figure 10, are from his book prepared for the Marquess of Bute in the Mount Stuart Library, Bute. Figures 19, 20, 21, 22, 37 and 38 are reproduced by permission of English Heritage, NMR, Swindon. Figure 15 is used by courtesy of Salisbury and South Wiltshire Museum. Figures 6, 7, 17 and 18, taken from the books by Hoare and Reed, were photographed by the publisher. Figures 26, 27 and 28 have been used with permission of the excavator, Dr Lawrence Butler. Other photographs were taken by my wife, Ann Thompson.

For advice or references I am indebted to Andrew Saunders, one-time Chief Inspector of Ancient Monuments; Sir Howard Colvin of St John's College Oxford; Burnard Nurse, Librarian of the Library of the Society of Antiquaries of London; Donald Moore of the National Library of Wales at Aberystwyth; and Peter Harbison, archaeologist to the Bord Failte in Dublin.

Abbreviations

CPS	Commons Preservation Society
DNB	*Dictionary of National Biography*
GPR	Thompson, *General Pitt-Rivers*
HMSO	Her Majesty's Stationery Office
JCH	Thompson, *Journals of Sir Richard Colt Hoare, 1793–1810*
NT	National Trust
PD (C)	*Parliamentary Debates (Commons)*
PD (L)	*Parliamentary Debates (Lords)*
RCHM	Royal Commission on Historic Monuments
SPAB	Society for the Protection of Ancient Buildings
VCH	*Victoria County History*
WWW	*Who Was Who*

Chapter 1

Introduction

Attitudes towards ruins have varied at different times; they can produce different effects on people according to temperament and their own particular interests, financial or otherwise, weather conditions, and most importantly, if they have an idea of the people who built the original buildings. They may cause positive dislike, indifference, curiosity, fear or even total absorption. What the present book is concerned with is not particular personal feelings but the slow appreciation that these remains can be used to understand, appreciate, respect or even admire those to whom the vestiges belong. This has taken a long time to mature and has been influenced by all sorts of extraneous factors which will be the main topics of the book.

There are one or two areas where there is often confusion between ruins and apparently analogous remains. Small portable antiquities including pictures are collectable and have been collected for centuries; anything that is collected can be bought or sold so there is a market, a vast one, for small antiquities. Many visitors to museums are more interested in the assumed cash value of the objects on display, particularly those of gold and silver, than in their value for telling us of the life of the people who made them. We all know the gasps of pleasure when owners are told on television of the value of their antiques. The looters of Baghdad were not primarily vandals; their aim was to carry off what they knew they could sell.[1] Museums are in a sense an extension from private to public collections, equally at the mercy of the market when making acquisitions. This influences the ethos of a museum or art gallery, for collecting on any scale is normally associated with the rich.

Ruins, on the other hand, are far too large to collect and are meaningless away from their original place of construction. Their cash value is normally zero or even a negative one because of the cost of propping them up or preserving them. There is no market for them and as a rule only the state can afford to collect them. It is not surprising that the maintenance of ruins in this country came in with the embryonic welfare state before the First World War.[2]

Ruins can be beautiful in their own right but are not usually attractive and are indeed often ugly and repellent. The art historian normally confines his attention to surviving buildings or ruins that are largely intact, like those cared for by the National Trust. The pleasure that Rose Macaulay gained from ruins was derived from allowing the imagination to play over a ruin upon which one has previously acquired a wide historical background. One has only to hear visitors on the site of a ruin discussing its merits with that of a stately home that they have recently visited to appreciate that the pictures, furniture, carpets and so on in a roofed building are held in far greater esteem. The visit to the ruin is made out of a sense of duty, curiosity or even patriotism.

Neither the market nor even aesthetics furnish ruins with friends. These friendless remains had to establish their value in their own right without the advantage of collectability, although recently, with the growth of worldwide travel, they have unexpectedly aquired a commercial interest, quite accidentally. This will have to be mentioned later as another factor in their preservation, but in this book the main interest is with development of an awareness of their inherent value on the one hand and, on the other, how this led to more or less successful attempts to preserve them.

On the face of it the preservation of fragmentary remains of ancient buildings, sometimes little more than footings and foundations, seems a very irrational thing to do. There are still many people who would feel this way now. With worldwide preservation of ruins growing exponentially one has to explain or justify this puzzling phenomenon as an extension of commercial tourism. By studying changing attitudes and motives of those who have tried to preserve them we may obtain some insight into the matter.

The author, who has spent much of his working life in a state organisation concerned with conservation, has seen things from the inside, as it were; so this book will be concerned with developments in this country, with only slight reference to events abroad. However, one cannot ignore the recently published translation of Mme Francoise Choay's *The Invention of the Historic Monument,* an invaluable account of what happened in France.[3] The French experience, where the Revolution caused vast numbers of royal, aristocratic and ecclesiastical buildings to come into the hands of the state and produced the expression 'monument historique', is utterly different from the British one, which gave rise to very different attitudes and legislation.

Protection of monuments in this country began with ruins, mainly prehistoric, in the 'Schedule' attached to the 1882 Act (Appendix 3). Historic Monument *(monument historique)* would have been an inappropriate title for these, so 'ancient monument' became the legal title. The traveller crossing the channel is surprised by the different designation but the differences go very much deeper, as will be evident in this book. As the word 'monument' is much used here it may be useful to define it now. In French and English it is borrowed from Latin *monumentum,* meaning a reminder recalling some event, person or feature of the past. A monument is meant to prompt or stir the memory, as is more evident in European languages where they have invented their own terms, like *Denkmal* in German or *pamyatnik* in Russian.

Ruins, when first seen, can give a shock and are difficult to ignore. The Old English poem about Roman ruins, perhaps at Bath,[4] is often quoted and no doubt the ruins in Rome prompted Gibbon to write *The Decline and Fall of the Roman Empire.* We have all experienced this kind of delicious melancholy at how the mighty have fallen and shared the feelings of Shelley about Ozymandias. No one doubts the pleasure derived from this experience but that is not the reason for legally designating a ruin a 'monument'!

The pioneers of legislation in this country, John Lubbock and Augustus Pitt-Rivers, were thinking in terms of monuments as evidence for steps in the advance of mankind, not at all the way medievalists a generation later looked at them. The point they had in common was that the remains were contemporary and unaltered evidence from the period of their original construction. It is the change from the ruin being a memory-jogger to a contemporary document, albeit difficult to read, that will be a theme of this book.

The object of designating a ruin as a monument is not just to give it that special status, but primarily to give it the protection that the status affords. In the generality of privately owned monuments this is merely negative; that is, prohibiting damage by an owner or developer. However, there is a substantial number of monuments in state care where the question of how they are to be treated and displayed arises. When I last wrote on this subject for British Museum Publications in 1981 the matter seemed resolved but the question of 'restoration' that so racked architects in the nineteenth century and was apparently resolved by the twentieth century is stirring again. It is a central one in all conservation and arouses fierce controversy, so the matter will crop up now and again in this book.

Ruins occur of course in most parts of the world, wherever people built durable structures and later abandoned them. One thinks of Classical ruins in the Mediterranean area which have aroused interest and study since the Renaissance and provided many elements for architects to copy. Sir Richard Colt Hoare, to whose activities the next chapter will be devoted, would no doubt have preferred to study Classical ruins in the Mediterranean area had not Revolutionary and Napoleonic wars prevented him going there, so causing him to turn his attention to Wales.

The abrupt and dramatic termination of the monasteries by Henry VIII created a

Figure 1 *Tattershall Castle keep*

class of widespread ruin that has aroused interest since the sixteenth century. Even in the twentieth century the Ministry of Works assumed them to be the monument *par excellence*, often ripe for taking into state care. In point of fact medieval castles, being of more solid construction, are more numerous and often larger than monastic remains. Medieval ruins tended to be the staple diet of public interest until a whole new category of ruin, industrial monuments, has challenged their primacy in recent years.

* * * * *

The recognition of the great antiquity of man in the nineteenth century has given that vast period without written records, and only documented by the remains themselves, a special interest. The ruins, if that is the right word, are mainly earthworks with no visible masonry (megalithic tombs or temples, like Stonehenge, are the exception) such as hill forts or burial mounds, which were indeed erected as monuments in a literal sense. They differ from normal ruins in that they require little or no expenditure on maintenance, a fundamental difference from an administrative point of view.

The discussion here will be episodic, with different chapters dealing with different aspects up until ancient monuments were put out to grass, so to speak, in 1984, separated from the state and handed over to independent Commissions: English Heritage in England, Historic Scotland in Scotland and *Cadw* in Wales.

The chapter following this is entitled 'Awareness'. As mentioned above, ruins impinged on the consciousness of later peoples in the same area, especially where they had a respect or reverence for the people who made them, as with Roman or monastic remains. The cultivated consciousness of Romanticism nourished the imagination; we need only think of the novels of Sir Walter Scott.[5] The searcher after the 'picturesque' confronted reality and in his state of mind ruins particularly aroused his interest, leading in the course of time to a much greater understanding of them.

One could no doubt comb the vast literature to illustrate this but I have chosen a concrete example in Sir Richard Colt Hoare (1758–1838), whose change from Classicist to Medievalist is well documented in his travel diaries[6] and in his own published account of the journey by Giraldus Cambrensis around Wales in 1188 with Archbishop Baldwin, recruiting for the third crusade.[7] Ruins were an important element in tracing this route and took over as an interest in themselves.

Hoare seems to have been quite indifferent to religion although he was interested in Gothic architecture, which merited a section in his work on Giraldus.[8] The religious revival of the 1820s entirely altered the attitude to Gothic architecture and, of course, ruins. It gave a great fillip to its study and led to the formation of two national and many county societies for whom it was their main topic of interest. Monastic ruins provided a feast of plans and mouldings to be recorded.

Even more important was the huge scale of church restoration that stemmed from this and which we see all over the country. Some churches had indeed been allowed to fall into ruin so restoration brought a former ruin back into use. From our point of view it was the struggles of conscience brought about by the aesthetics of Ruskin that raised the value of the original masonry to an almost sacred historical level, as if part of a manuscript. So all restored masonry became false, almost indeed an evil deception. The Society for Protection of Ancient Buildings formed by William Morris in 1877 was intended to protect ancient buildings from restoration, not from the weather or demolition or damage! The whole attitude towards preservation of built structures in this country as will be seen in Chapter 2, has been moulded by Ruskin and Morris.[9]

Another matter having its origins in religious conscience was the disestablishment of the Church of Ireland; the vast majority of the inhabitants of Ireland were Roman Catholics. As part of the agreement in the Act of 1869, the ruins belonging to the former Irish Church were transferred to the Irish Board of Works. This was not only an acknowledgement by the Government that it had a responsibility in this field but also created a precedent for the similar department at Westminster to take on this liability. Ireland was referred to by Lubbock in the Commons debates and others must have been well aware of the events.

Our fourth chapter deals with one of the most fascinating episodes of late nineteenth century: the intervention of two men, both claiming to be scientists, in the formation and implementation of legislation to protect ancient monuments. One was Sir John Lubbock, later Lord Avebury (his title referring to the great earthwork), a banker who wrote works of popular science and on the (recently recognised) prehistory of man.[10] The other, General A.H. Pitt-Rivers, was a soldier by profession but a collector of mainly ethnographic material and in later life a great excavator of archaeological sites.[11] Pitt-Rivers, Lane-Fox as he then was, had started collecting at the time of the Great Exhibition of 1851 with the aim of arranging objects in a series to illustrate their development, and found a powerful analogy with the evolution of living things as propounded by Darwin. As Darwin signed his proposal form for the Royal Society he cannot have regarded it as all nonsense.[12] Lubbock was a personal friend of Darwin while Pitt-Rivers had dealings through the Ethnological Society with Thomas Huxley, who tried to persuade the South Kensington Museum to retain his collection.

Emboldened by the popularity of his Bank Holiday Act, in the 1870s Lubbock (a Liberal MP) introduced repeatedly a private Bill to protect ancient monuments, mainly prehistoric ones. His successive attempts came close but failed; on the return of Gladstone to power in 1880 a Government Bill based on an emasculated form of Lubbock's passed into law. Pitt-Rivers was responsible for implementing it as the statutory Inspector of Ancient Monuments, paid part-time (1883–90) and honorary until his death. He carried out the great excavations in Cranborne Chase at the same time.

Although it is not unusual to sneer at the Lubbock/Pitt-Rivers episode this is too harsh. The archaeological fieldwork aspect of conservation so evident with us today and absent in France owes much to Pitt-Rivers, who created a sort of private organisation. Their weakness was that they thought in museum terms of full acquisition of the monuments by a commission or museum. A criticism in Parliament was that they excluded the large but costly medieval monuments and that Lubbock was trying to advance his special interest in prehistoric moments, as no doubt he was. The two fundamental weaknesses were, first, the absence of compulsory powers (not Lubbock's fault), if only to hold in reserve and, second, a method of designating structures as protected without actually taking them over ('scheduling' in the modern jargon). Neither of these matters were put right until 1913 – a subject addressed in Chapter 5.

We cannot leave the nineteenth century without mentioning voluntary bodies and more especially the National Trust.[13] Founded originally to preserve common land this was expanded to include buildings and places of natural beauty, which might include ruins. Its admirable work really came into full flower when the arrival of the motor car allowed the public to visit the great country houses in its ownership. This subject is an enthralling one but outside the scope of this book.

Chapter 5 is entitled 'Imperial Responsibilities – Lord Curzon', and refers to his work in India together with other matters that led up to the 1913 Act (repealed 1979) which still lies at the root of most thinking in this field. There had been minor legislation since 1882 giving powers of acquisition to Local Authorities and extending the term to include medieval monuments. The most significant move in preparation for possible legislation was the creation of a Royal Commission to survey the counties and create inventories of historic monuments from which those suitable for preservation might be selected; that is, to measure the extent of the problem. In fact, in its 90 years of existence, it collected an invaluable record and archive in its inventories and other additional material on buildings and other monuments.

The government took other steps to prepare for legislation such as having translations made of legislation on this topic at the embassies in Paris and Vienna. It was indeed at something of a loss over how to proceed when two new factors moved matters forward, both of which had imperial overtones. The first of these was not a Liberal but a Conservative, the arch-Imperialist, Lord Curzon.[14]

Curzon, in his period as Viceroy of India, had created a successful Ancient Monuments Department with its own Director General and promoted Indian legislation on the subject, so was the only politician with first-hand experience in this field.[15] Furthermore, from his youth, he had had a keen interest in grand (Muslim) architecture which he had encountered during his travels. After his return to England in 1905 his headship of the Irish peers (1908), later Earl of Kedleston, gave him a seat in the Lords.

The great fifteenth-century tower at Tattershall Castle, Lincolnshire, was calculated to arouse his enthusiasm. It was advertised for sale in 1911 after the famous mantelpieces had been taken out, giving rise to a patriotic outcry (Figure 1). Events can be followed in the Times. Curzon made a lightning personal visit to Tattershall and telegraphed an offer to the owners that was accepted.[16] The mantelpieces were hidden in London awaiting dispatch to America; they were located, pressure brought to bear on the holders and returned in triumph to Tattershall. The state had been exposed as entirely impotent under the existing law, while the National Trust, in spite of the offer of a loan, could not afford to purchase the castle. Curzon's intervention at this time must be regarded as at least in part politically motivated.

The Bill was introduced in the House of Lords by the First Commissioner of Works who, at that date, was Earl Beauchamp. The Bill's support in one of Curzon's notable speeches referred of course to Tattershall. The rather hesitant tone of the First Commissioner seemed to imply that the Bill was provisional and left much undone. Whether there would have been legislation before the First World War without the pressure from Curzon one may doubt.

The other 'imperial' factor was the brainchild of Lloyd George, namely the spectacular ceremony of the Investiture of the Prince of Wales at Caernarvon Castle in 1911. It suddenly brought a great monument to the fore, as the account in the *Times* makes clear, but, even more important, Works staff recruited for preparing the castle for this event moved eastward from Caernavon to tackle the growing number of monuments in care (116 in 1912, 140 in 1913). Indeed, Caernarvon Castle was a major depot into the 1920s.

The only certain matter in the mind of Government was that this was a 'Works' matter, a sort of extension of a department that had already existed since medieval times, an organisation that already dealt with medieval monuments like the Tower of London, Hampton Court and so on. This is fundamentally different from France, where the whole medieval apparatus was swept away at the Revolution and they could start with a *tabula rasa*. It is crucial to understanding the course of events and why, incidentally, Lubbock was keen to have a separate Commission.

The much-contested compulsory powers were supplied by Preservation Orders giving powers of compulsory guardianship, a compromise measure, with fines for not giving notice of work on a scheduled site. The schedule at the end of the 1882 Act was to be expanded indefinitely, the new form of designation by the First Commissioner on the advice of advisory Boards in England and Wales, the first step in complete geographical division. 'Inhabited' buildings and churches were excluded, only being protected by planning legislation at the end of the Second World War. This meant in effect that, apart from bridges and a few other categories, most scheduled monuments were either ruins or earthworks from all periods. The ingenious system of 'guardianship' was a face-saving device, which left the freehold to the owner but put control of the monument into the hands of the Office of Works.

The sixth chapter is concerned with State preservation. The now rapidly increasing number of scheduled monuments, counted by thousands, and of monuments in care, counted by hundreds, is a mundane matter that one cannot describe to arouse interest. The variation in kind between simple standing stones to large castles or monasteries makes most statistics fairly meaningless. The division between England, Scotland and Wales became increasingly sharper and was virtually total by the 1970s, with separate ministers responsible for each country.

After the death of General Pitt-Rivers in 1900 the statutory post remained unfilled until 1910 when an architect, Charles Peers (later Sir Charles Peers), was appointed. This indicated a change of direction. He was the only architect who held the post between 1880 and its recent termination, the others being archaeologists.[17] How much credit attaches to Peers and how much to Sir Frank Baines, the Director of the Office of Works, for laying down the principles on which the monuments were displayed it is difficult to say, although much credit is normally given to Baines.

The running of the organisation was done as an isosceles triangle, two professional groups of architects and inspectors with an administrator controlling the money and indeed in overall control. This could lead to friction and one of the happier outcomes of the creation of the Commission, English Heritage, is that it now seems (2006) to have become a professional organisation. The large body of direct labour, including craftsmen, scattered over the country and the basic element in the whole organisation came under the control of the architects. This allowed a high degree of uniformity to be achieved over the whole country, a characteristic feature of the English monuments in care.

Leaving aside the designation of monuments, 'scheduling' as it was called, the more mundane of the activities associated with ancient monuments, producing a list that has grown exponentially since 1913, it is to the treatment of monuments in care that attention is turned, which has resulted in those very characteristic sights all over the country with their sombre grey masonry and mown grass. The first point to make is that their appearance has been very materially altered by exposure of a great deal of masonry, formerly covered by vegetation or buried by the accumulated debris around the base. This can reach as much as one or two metres deep so that its removal can transform scrappy visible remains into sizeable walls. The actual treatment of the masonry, its consolidation, can only be carried out when all the surviving stonework is visible. The other crucial point is to establish where the ruin belongs in the overall plan of the monastery, castle or other group of buildings so that it is intelligible as part of a whole.

The two key objectives of the treatment, apart from stabilising the structure, are to retain all original masonry without trying to add to it or falsify the evidence and to render the surviving part as intelligible as possible in relation to the original building. In point of fact it may be necessary to replace materials such as wood in rafters in a roof or restore a roof to protect painted plaster, delicate mouldings and so on. Where something is missing that is crucial to the plan one can mark out with materials so as not to deceive.[18]

The details of, for instance, mortar mix, the proportions of lime to sand or, in the carpentry, the use of wooden pegs in medieval fashion for securing beams derive from the strong arts and craft Morris tradition that was in vogue at the time they were first adopted, just before the First World War when the Office of Works was feeling its way forward. It is easier to understand what one sees if one understands the intentions of the people who did the work. Some more exuberant work in the style of Viollet-le-Duc by Burges will have been discussed earlier.[19] It was of course not possible and most might say not desirable for a Government Department to emulate the extravagances of the Marquess of Bute.

The rising cost of labour has profoundly affected the work on ancient monuments, which grew up with cheap labour, and some of the early work, particularly the large-scale clearance of sites, has become prohibitively expensive. There is indeed now a tendency to use contract labour but the merits and demerits of contract as opposed to direct labour is not a subject that one can discuss here.

Another development owing its origins to the Second World War has been rescue excavation, carried out first on the site of proposed aerodromes and then growing exponentially to embrace all threats from development or agriculture. This is now carried out outside Government, which provides some support services. It was a cruder affair in the 1950s, when the present author carried out and published some nine excavations not, as done now, with a skilled workforce. It is a quite fascinating subject best described by someone involved in it, since it is only indirectly relevant to standing ruins.

Since the Planning Acts have brought inhabited buildings within schemes of preservation depending largely on Local Authorities, there has tended to be a slowly developed linkage between the bodies operating under the different types of legislation, largely amalgamated in the new Commissions. The listing of historic buildings has a hierarchical system of grades quite in contrast to the simple 'scheduling' classification. This fascinating subject deserves separate treatment. Unlike ruins, intact inhabited buildings have rarely been a matter for direct Government intervention.

So far as ruins are concerned, it is the constant advance forward of their dates which allows them to qualify as ancient monuments that has caused an enormous expansion in their numbers. To regard a wartime pillbox as an ancient monument might be regarded as laughable but by 1980 pillboxes were being scheduled. Perhaps the greatest increase has been caused by the recognition of industrial monuments from the Industrial Revolution as worthy of preservation. They require quite different treatment from traditional monuments; machinery has to be made to work and protected from the weather. This brings into the field a new type of engineering enthusiast and also new visitors, particularly children. This is not within the scope of this book.

We have seen how collectable objects preserve themselves, their value allowing them to float as it were on a permanent market. Politics hardly comes into it except where there may be a sudden fit of conscience about their removal from their places of origin, as with the Elgin Marbles. With ruins there is no market and preservation money has to come either from Government or what one can take from visitors. Politics comes into the matter straight away.

* * * * *

It has been accident that has brought Government into the matter in the beginning, for example with the great mass of buildings forfeited to the state at the French Revolution or the mass of ruins deposited with the Irish Board of Works after 1869. I want, finally, to leave the state out as far as one can and look at the motives and social attitudes of some of the people involved; and we may start with Colt Hoare, who was active long before any Government involvement.

In the Romantic 'Enlightenment' period, if Colt Hoare may be regarded as its representative, curiosity was the reason for having Cunnington open hundreds of burial mounds on Salisbury Plain without specific intention to preserve. Nevertheless the belief that the objects found could tell us something of the history of the people who made them is surely an advance.[20] Significantly, Hoare's trips to Wales started first. In Wales, Giraldus Cambrensis may have provided a guidebook to start with but ruins could define the places he halted at with all the history that flowed from this leading, of course, to Hoare's two-volume edition of Giraldus. Hoare may have been distressed by falls of masonry between his Welsh visits but he only emphasised the decay that was taking place. His curiosity and grasp of the value of ruins is what impresses.

Lubbock and Pitt-Rivers had no doubt about the reasons for preservation; the monuments were the evidence for the antiquity of man, one of the great discoveries of the nineteenth century. Both men had a slightly missionary side, Lubbock as a popular science writer and Pitt-Rivers in his well-known efforts to attract the public to the Farnham Museum, Dorset. The museum started life as a proposed school for gypsies but voluntary schools of this kind were rendered superfluous by the flow of legislation on compulsory primary education between 1870 and 1902 and the creation of County Councils to implement this, which was also no doubt responsible for the dramatic change in plan at Farnham from school to museum.[21]

The 1913 Act may have been part of the Liberal reforms but was in fact started in a fairly reluctant upper house impelled forward by the personal inclinations and successful experience in India of Lord Curzon, strengthened by Lloyd George's outburst of historicism at Caernarvon. Lloyd George, who started his political life as a strong Welsh nationalist, had his own reasons for promoting the 1911 Investiture.[22]

There has been a patriotic element in preservation, as is apparent in the events connected with Tattershall, which permeates preservation at home and abroad. A new financial element has been introduced by the easy accessibility due to universal motor transport. In the eyes of politicians monuments have become an extension of the tourist industry, not just in Britain but world-wide. In some countries tourism is the main industry. Television is incessantly thrusting monuments forward in all sorts of contexts. More and more efforts are being made to render them intelligible. Blandishments like car parks and toilets are being conferred on the larger ones while the smaller ones tend to be left in lonely neglect. The present writer does not disapprove of this; if we wish to preserve them on theoretical grounds then the more they are used the better. Only if their fabric is harmed by the blandishments, as might be the case with over-zealous restoration, does the need for protest really arise.

Notes

1 In the case of Baghdad it turned out that much more had been hidden by the curators than had been supposed.
2 The 1913 Act really started or, at all events, authorised the preservation of ruins on a large scale.
3 Choay 2000, first published in French in 1992.
4 Thompson 1981, 13.
5 *ibid*, 15.
6 Thompson 1983.
7 Hoare 1806.
8 *ibid,* Vol II, 413–33.
9 See chapter 3 with references.
10 See chapter 4 with references.
11 Thompson 1977.
12 *ibid*. The Librarian of the Royal Society kindly supplied me with a photocopy of Pitt-Rivers's candidature certificate.
13 Murphy 1987: a fuller account in Fedden 1968.
14 See chapter 5 with references.
15 There are a number of biographies, the official one being by the Earl of Ronaldshay, 1928, 3 vols.
16 See p.52 below.
17 See chapter 6. Biographical material for Sir Frank Baines (1877–1933) and Sir Charles Peers (1868–1952) in *WWW* after their deaths.
18 Thompson 1981.
19 *ibid,*18–19.
20 Hoare 1812–21.
21 Thompson and Renfrew 1999.
22 Owen 1955.

Chapter 2

Awareness – Colt Hoare

The name of Richard Colt Hoare is familiar to archaeologists from his association with William Cunnington in the 'opening' of hundreds of burial mounds in Wiltshire and his two-volume work, *The Ancient History of Wiltshire,* as well as the unfinished *Modern History of Wiltshire.*[1] Visitors to Stourhead, the great house in Wiltshire in which Hoare lived, which is now in the hands of the National Trust, will have seen the superb library he constructed there; only the shelves and fittings now survive for, alas, the books were sold in the nineteenth century. Fortunately a catalogue had been published[2] which makes record of two sets of manuscript volumes, one quarto and one folio, that describe his various daily experiences on his journeys in search of the picturesque, mainly in Wales and to a less extent in England and Ireland in 1793–1810. The folios were written up as fair copy possibly with the intention of publication. Both sets are now in Cardiff City Library. I have transcribed a very abbreviated version from the quartos, which is frequently quoted in this chapter.[3]

Hoare, who was of a wealthy banking family, had travelled extensively on the Continent in his youth, particularly in Italy as far south as Sicily. The outbreak of the French Revolutionary wars in 1793, the year our diaries begin, prevented continental travel and the journeys to Wales were to some extent a substitute. The 'tourist' in pursuit of the picturesque was a familiar figure in the period, attracted by the 'coquetry' of nature, to use Hoare's phrase, so there was nothing odd about such journeys. Hoare, because of his wealth, could travel in some style, usually partly by carriage and partly on horseback. He did not, unlike George Borrow later on, go on foot. He travelled often with a learned companion and stayed with friends or at inns and, eventually, in his own 'villa' overlooking Lake Bala.

Before he went to Wales, Hoare knew Wyndham, one of the earliest Welsh tourists, who lived in Salisbury,[4] and had been influenced by him particularly by his use, as a guidebook, of the *Itinerary* of Giraldus Cambrensis describing his journey around Wales in 1188 ; Hoare was to publish a two-volume edition of this work to which we will refer often.[5] He was also influenced by Thomas Pennant, a native Welshman, a naturalist of distinction and topographer of London and Scotland whose three volumes of *Tours in Wales* (only north Wales) appeared shortly before Hoare went there.[6] William Coxe, a Cambridge historian and traveller in Eastern Europe, who Hoare accompanied in 1799 to do the drawings for Coxe's *Historical Tour of Monmouthshire,* was probably the main influence on Hoare in implanting in his mind the intention to make an edition of Giraldus that would constitute a sort of *Historical Tour of Wales*.[7] Richard Fenton, a friend and pupil of Hoare published *Historical Tour of Pembrokeshire in 1811*.[8] The historical tour of a county in Wales was perhaps the nearest thing to an English county history.

Hoare's travel diaries are in no sense private diaries recording personal feelings and problems of the journey. We do not even know if he was travelling alone from the diary although other sources may show that he had a companion. The diaries are selective, only written on journeys where he sought and consciously laid himself open to the picturesque 'experience'. This might be caused by chance, by a natural feature or where he made a detour to see, for example, a waterfall; to produce the experience, not only natural but artificial features might catch his eye. These could be entirely modern, especially those with a great deal of movement. He found the Blaenavon blast furnaces with their flame and smoke, which he drew for Coxe, particularly exciting.[9] The Parys copper mines which he explored in Anglesey he found very impressive.[10] Telford's canal aqueducts under construction at the time of his visits also excited him (Figure 3). The modern industrial archaeologist would share many feelings with him. Ruins were in some sense the bread and butter of his excursions and in these there were at least three different matters to take into account.

Some readers may have visited Cilgerran Castle and, from the two magnificent thirteenth-century towers, stared down into the dark, mysterious and heavily-wooded valley of the River Teifi. Hoare recommended looking up from a boat in the river when of course the towers of the ruin would be outlined against the sky; we may share Hoare's view that it would be one of most picturesque and sublime views that Wales has to offer:

Figure 2 *Hoare's drawing of Teifi river valley*

No description can give an adequate idea of the beautiful scenery on the banks of this river, nor could the most ingenious artist or the man of greatest taste have placed a ruin in a more happy spot...[11]

How different is the appearance of the castle on the landside! It might almost be passed by unnoticed; whereas by water it forms the grandest and most pleasing ruin in South Wales and cannot fail to leave a lasting impression on the recollection of every traveller who visits it.[12]

The two quotes are from 1793 and 1802: in the first Hoare speaks in purely picturesque terms as if the scene were a picture, whereas later he went up to the ruin and examined the towers themselves, even if he was not very impressed by them. The second point is that Hoare regarded himself as an artist and part of the object of the visit was to make a drawing of the ruin, rather as the modern tourist takes a photograph. Scores of his drawings survive, many published, the main collection being in the National Library of Wales in Aberystwyth. Some are used in this book. The sketches are not of the highest quality and do not bear comparison with watercolours of the young William Turner painted at about the same time as Hoare was in Wales. Hoare commissioned work from Turner, but of English subjects.[13]

The third matter to be mentioned is the historical nature of the ruin. After his journey with Coxe in 1799 to Monmouthshire, the historical aspect of ruins was his main interest and, as he traced the route taken by Giraldus, he concerned himself with their particular associations. He had the usual problem of how to date the visible remains; although he published an elaborate chronological system by Carter in the second volume of the *Itinerary*, he may not have understood it and used it.[14] It was nearly always the 'drawability' of the monument that was his main consideration. This applied especially to castles; with the church building of a monastery he was far more at home although he had no understanding of the conventual buildings associated with them.

We have seen his interest in industries in active use:

I descended the salt mines at Northwich... I cannot say without some degree of apprehension... Into one of these buckets two members of the party placed themselves attended by one of the miners. We seated ourselves on the edge of the bucket and the miner stood on the edge of it holding the rope... No words can convey an idea adequate to the surprise and admiration I felt on my first landing in these subterraneous abodes...[15]

With regard to large country houses, he was more interested in their grounds if they had been laid out in picturesque fashion but, if they were not, he was disappointed. Of Powis Castle he remarked in 1799:

With every local advantage which an elevated situation commanding a distant view over a rich and fertile plain bounded by high mountains can afford this building is not in itself a picturesque or very striking object. It arises from its little extent in length, the multitude of high narrow chimneys...[16]

He did not describe the two or three English cathedrals he visited but commented unfavourably on Wyatt's restoration work at Hereford and Durham. Of the former he wrote:

The effect and solemnity of the cathedral much injured by its being painted a dead white. The upper rows of arches over the Saxon (added by Mr Wyatt) are much too light in their construction...[17]

Figure 3 *Chirk Aqueduct under construction, drawn by Hoare.*

This hostility towards Wyatt evidently echoed the hostility of John Carter and the Society of Antiquaries.

Before turning to his edition of Giraldus, it may be helpful to quote some further views on ruins. Conwy Castle, as we might expect, aroused Hoare's enthusiasm:

> This magnificent castle appears to great advantage wherever it is viewed but the best points of view are from the fine woods of oak leading up the hill to Mr Pryor's house.[18]

That was in 1797; in 1801 he was still in picturesque mode:

> The four smaller towers annexed to the larger ones (and which served as their staircases) give a great air of lightness and elegance to the building...[19]

Tintern Abbey was a favourite, almost obligatory, tourist stop on the river trip from Hay to Chepstow:

> The old ferryman... He says that the clearing rubbish from the building cost the Duke of Beaufort £150. I wish he had still completed the improvement by removing the cottages and orchards around the building.[20]

In his journey of 1800 he compared Tintern with Kirkstall Abbey near Leeds:

> I was glad to find workmen repairing the old walls. Much might be done to add to the beautiful appearance of this abbey by clearing out the rubbish from the inside and thereby rendering it neat. Many have condemned the neat and trim changed appearance of Tintern Abbey, but I am sure no one with one grain of sentiment or feeling ever entered that building without strong sensations of pleasure and admiration...[21]

At Llandaff Cathedral he commented on the Norman doorways:

West front of the old cathedral bears a picturesque appearance. It is in a state of ruin. Three doors of Saxon architecture remain…[22]

The ruin he visited most often was Llanthony Priory in Monmouthshire, the fourth visit already in 1798:

The architecture is grand and simple. The breadth and massive appearance of the tower has a good effect in the midst of the Vale and well relieved by the mountains in the background…[23]

Seeing it frequently made Hoare aware of the rapidity of decay, in 1803:

Weather fine. Visited once more and probably for the last time the ruins of Llanthony Abbey, which are alas, approaching rapidly to dissolution. I was informed that last year a part of the fine Gothic windows in the western front had given way, and now I had the sad mortification to find that all these three elegant windows (by far the most elegant part of the window) had in the preceding winter fallen to the ground… the chapter house at Margam is now no more and Llanthony will soon no longer excite nor deserve the attention of the traveller.

The reference is to the polygonal chapter house at Margam Abbey, which still had its vault when seen by Hoare in 1793.[24] In 1802:

That chef d'oeuvre of elegant Gothic architecture is, alas, no more and every passing traveller will weep over its sad relicts… And how little care would have preserved it for many centuries in its original state of perfection?…[25]

The two cases of Llanthony and Margam demonstrate the awareness of Hoare of major falls of masonry between visits and that 'a little care and trifling expence' might have prevented it. He assumed that this was the owner's responsibility.

That he had changed his attitude from disdain to admiration for native antiquities over the ten years he had been visiting Wales is shown by the remark he made in 1802:

Few villages are more delightfully situated than Crickhowell. I reviewed with pleasure the spot where in 1793 I had spent so many pleasant days. My ardour for monumental antiquities had not then begun, nor had I ever seen the inside of the church.[26]

Figure 4 *Sketch of Goodrich Castle by Hoare.*

While travelling in England in 1800 he made a revealing remark:

> My pencil has at last had a day of rest. Castles and abbeys have furnished it with employment, and in such rapid succession since I left the mountains of Cumberland... These ancient buildings may be called the guides and landmarks of history. They animate the artist's picture and often induce the tourist to trace their origin, their architecture, their history; by them he by degrees gains a daily knowledge of his country. Independent of the ornament and resources it affords the love of drawing has more essential advantages. The Man of Taste, gifted with a picturesque eye, views every object with double pleasure: every tint, every shadow, in short every object in nature affords employment to the mind. Nothing remains to him unobserved for even in the dullest of countries something may be learnt by the steady observance of nature.[27]

The language may be slightly pompous, even snobbish, but the general truth of the observation is surely not open to doubt. An interest in the picturesque enhances awareness of the surroundings. Ruins stand out as something not natural to that environment, picturesque no doubt, but also requiring explanation. It gives dignity to those rather sorry remains and you cannot think about preserving them until you hold them in respect.

Hoare did not confine his interest to medieval monuments but was interested also in the scanty Roman remains that he encountered as well as in megalithic tombs. In 1797:

> Caerwent: an old Roman station on a slight eminence surrounded by a square wall of great thickness. Great part of it remains and surrounds in part the churchyard and orchard where the Roman pavement was discovered...[28]

In 1801 in Anglesey:

> At Trevawr (Trevor) saw a perfect cromlech in a cornfield on left of the roadside.[29]

* * * * *

From 1793, the journey to Wales started from Stourhead, going north and crossing the Severn on the ferry, but a few years later he established a more permanent base overlooking Lake Bala from the south side. The date of construction of his 'villa' is not certain but a later writer says its cost was shared with Sir John Leicester of Tabley, Cheshire, a fellow patron of the arts with whom he had enjoyed a lifelong friendship since they met in Italy in 1786.[30] He first saw Lake Bala in 1796[31] and in June 1797 evidently spent some time there, riding around the lake and attracted by the fishing and the possibility of hiring a boat for this activity.[32] He found the village of Bala 'something picturesque...one long, wide street with some sycamore trees projecting into it.'[33] He disliked the inn and it is possible that he decided to buy a house facing the lake at that time; the idea of constructing a sort of pavilion parallel to the lake was clearly suggested by what he saw in the Lake District near Derwent Water in his trip there in 1800:

> ... the little retired villa of Lord William Gordon which is built on the ground with one storey only in a sequestered bay and so much enveloped with wood that you can scarcely discern it...It commands a delicious view of the lake without itself being commanded...[34]

It is possible that it was constructed very soon after because, by 1805, Hoare speaks of 'my shady retreat at Vachdeiliog' and in 1808 'Returned to Vachdeiliog' (Fach Ddeiliog,

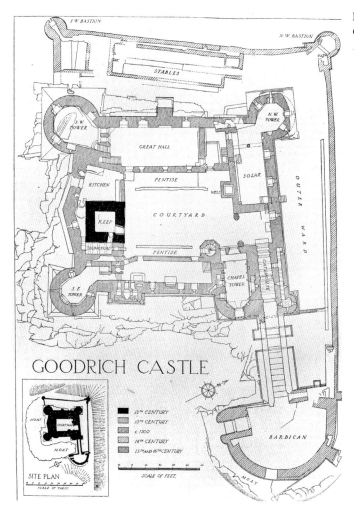

Figure 5 *Plan of Goodrich Castle after retrieval in the 1920s. See fig 4.*

little leafy spot).[35] He seems to have used the 'villa' until he lost interest in Wales after the end of the Napoleonic Wars.

Figure 9, drawn by Hoare himself, shows a large bungalow-style building with central bow window and a verandah with cast iron supports running round the sides and front of the building. According to our later source it consisted of a central hall measuring 30 by 24 feet with smaller bedroom and parlour at either end.[36] Apart from services it is vaguely medieval in plan, the services presumably being in the two-storeyed house behind, said to have been used for servants. Hoare makes no reference to Leicester using it but this may not have been the case. Now part of a motel, it is of some architectural interest as an early bungalow-style structure, not a 'cottage ornée'.

The 'villa' was well situated in central north Wales to reach most monuments and in 1806 Hoare set out from here on his trip to Ireland, the results of which were published in 1807.[37] The text of this is in the quarto volume but, as we might expect, not in the folios.

* * * * *

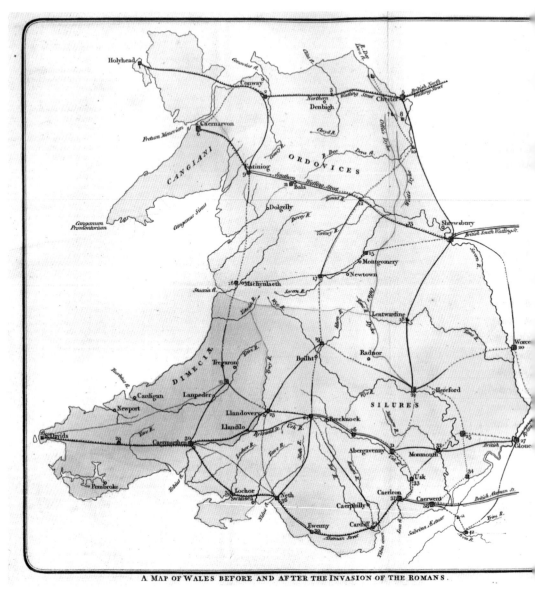

A MAP OF WALES BEFORE AND AFTER THE INVASION OF THE ROMANS.

Out of a very prolific volume of writing by Giraldus Cambrensis, a native of west Wales, of the two works on Wales the *Itinerary* was far more useful topographically than the *Description*. Most of the places mentioned could be identified on a contemporary map and the route taken by Baldwin, Archbishop of Canterbury, whom Giraldus accompanied on his recruiting drive, followed the coast through the most densely inhabited areas, Welsh and English. As a guidebook it had quite a lot to commend it. Having decided, perhaps when he was with Coxe in 1799,[38] to use it as a basis for the work in two great volumes that he published in 1806, a great deal of library work, as much as field work, was required.[39]

The original Latin text of Giraldus had been published by Hoare before the translation. Each book of Giraldus is accompanied by copious notes far larger than the original and

A TABLE OF REFERENCE

1	Caer Gybi	Holyhead.
2	Conovium	Caer Hen on the Conwy.
3	Varis	near Bodfari not far from Denbigh.
4		Flint.
5	Deva	Chester.
6	Segontium	Caer Seiont near Caernarvon.
7		Caergwrle.
8		Holt.
9	Heriri Mons	Tommen y mur near Festiniog.
10	Banchorium	Banchor on the Dee.
11		Caer Gai near Bala.
12	Mediolanum	on the Tanad.
13	Rutunium	Rowton.
14	Uriconium	Wroxeter.
15		Gaer near Montgomery.
16		Penalt near Machynlaeth.
17		Caersws near Newtown.
18	Bravinium	near Lentwardine.
19		on the Ython.
20	Brannogena	near Worcester.
21	Luentium	Llanio isau.
22	Magna	Kenchester near Hereford.
23		Llanvair ar y brin near Llandovery.
24		Gaer near Brecknock.
25	Ariconium	at Bolitre near Rofs.
26		Gaer at Cwm Du.
27	Glevum	Gloucester.
28	Menapia	Saint Davids.
29	Adviesimum	Castel Fleming.
30	Maridunum	Caermarthen.
31	Gobannium	Abergavenny.
32	Blestium	Monmouth.
33	Burrium	Usk.
34		Lydney.
35	Leucarum	Lochor.
36	Nidum	Neath.
37	Isca Silurum	Caerleon.
38	Venta Silurum	Caerwent.
39	Bovium	near Ewenny.
40	Tibia Amnis	near Cardiff.
41	Ad Sabrinam	on the Borders of the Severn.
42	Abone	Sea Mills near Bristol.

EXPLANATION.

1	British Towns	▣
2	D.º Track-Ways	Black Line ———
3	Roman Stations certain	■
4	D.º D.º uncertain	▪
5	Roman Roads still existing	———
6	D.º D.º but their Track not	....
	absolutely known	
7	D.º D.º uncertain but probable	....
8	Watts & Offas Dikes	Green Line ———

Figure 6 *Map of Wales before and after the Roman conquest, by Hoare.*

is preceded by a life of Giraldus, an account of surviving manuscripts and an account of Roman Wales with a map (Figure 6). The Itinerary is followed by 'An Account of Owain Cyveilioc, Prince of Powys', a translation of the *Description* of Giraldus, a supplement of places omitted by Giraldus and finally 'The Progress of Architecture from the time of William the Conqueror to the Sixteenth Century', with drawings by John Carter.[40]

The last item is of particular interest because it reflects a complete break with the mocking attitude towards 'Gothick' of the Strawberry Hill style of Horace Walpole. Gothic architecture had its divisions (Class the first, Class the second…) and could be analysed in the same way as the Orders of Classical architecture. This was only a few years before Rickman devised the terminology that we use today. Hoare did not use the scheme devised by Carter in his diary, no doubt because of its cumbersomeness.

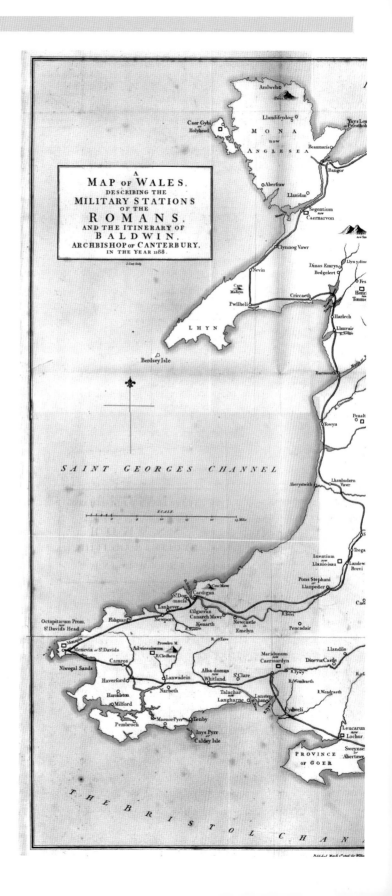

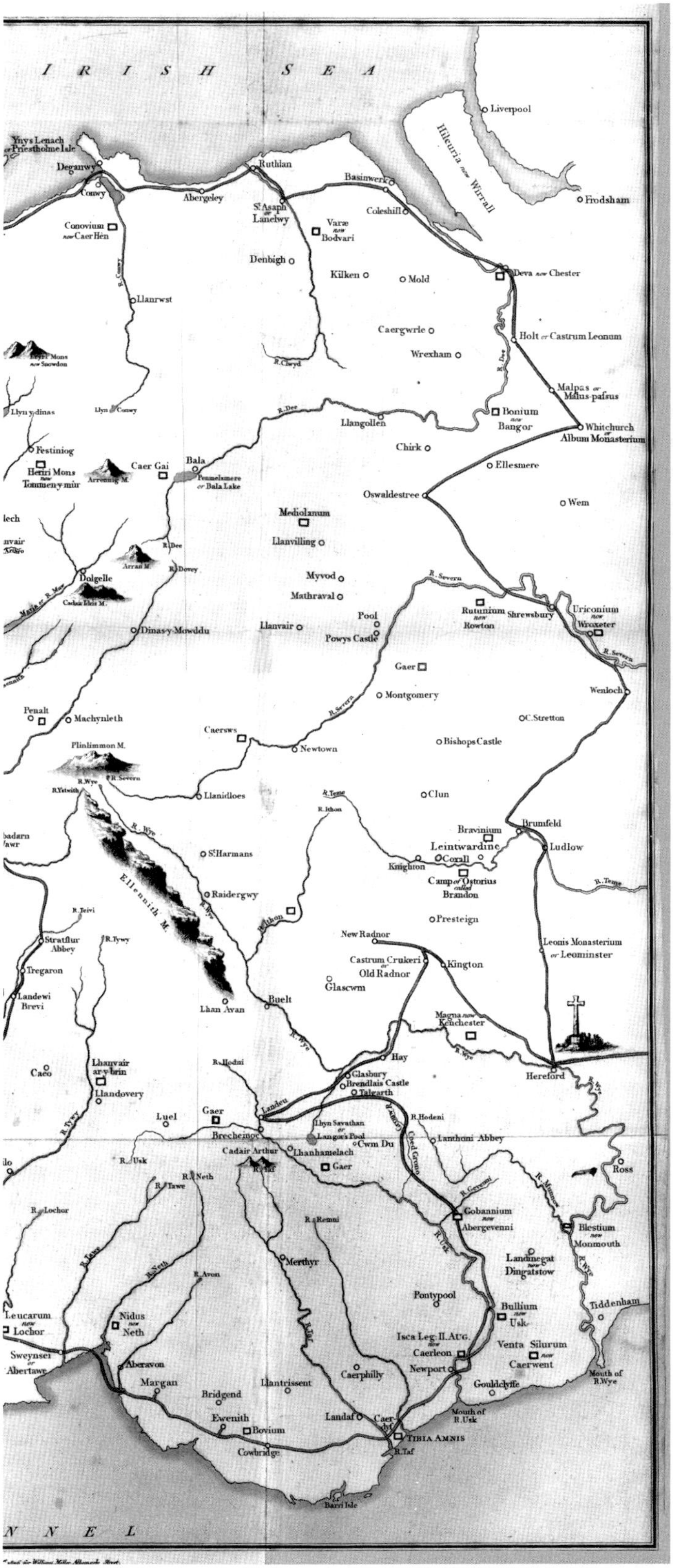

Figure 7 *Map of archbishop Baldwin's recruiting tour in 1188, by Hoare.*

There are 59 illustrations, including two maps, mainly, as we might expect, drawings by Hoare himself. It would be tedious to work through the book discussing the parts one by one, but the two maps show the state of knowledge of ruins or monuments at that time.

The first map, opposite page *cxli,* is entitled 'A Map of Wales before and after the Invasion of the Romans' (Figure 6). The four tribal areas, the 'before' part of the title of the map, are marked in different colours. Some 41 Roman stations are listed with Latin names where identifiable. Only a handful of these had visible remains, masonry or earthworks. The main courses of the Roman roads were known, if shown a little schematically. The level of knowledge of Roman Wales in 1806 is impressive. The 'British' towns are modern Welsh towns, not hillforts!

Now we may turn to the end of volume 2 for 'A Map of Wales describing the Military Stations of the Romans and the Itinerary of Baldwin Archbishop of Canterbury in the Year 1188' (Figure 7). The Roman stations are shown as little red squares and the modern towns and villages as black circles. The course taken by Baldwin is shown by a thick pink line. It is a pity there are no arrows to show the direction. Baldwin started at Hereford and then, crossing towards Radnor, went around Wales in a clockwise direction. The route started towards the south, then turned westwards along the south coast, northwards up the west coast, eastwards along the north coast as far as Chester and then southwards along the English side of the border to Ludlow and Hereford.

Its course can be measured out in ruinous abbeys and castles, sometimes associated with a modern town but often, like the important Cistercian abbeys of Whitland and Strata Florida, ruins or just humps and bumps in the grass. Most of the ruins were living structures in 1188 but, not unsurprisingly in the text, Hoare used his drawings of Edwardian castles or later items. As one runs one's eye along the route, ruin after ruin come to mind, sometimes vestiges of places where the party stayed for one or more nights. It seems to give an historical or enhanced status to the ruin.

* * * * *

When all is said and done, what did Hoare achieve? His picturesque approach appears old-fashioned and uninformative compared with the splendid surveys by John Britton discussed below. Yet by concentrating on a single dramatic historical event he seems to bring us closer to the ruined monuments. Hoare's English translations of Giraldus have been used in popular editions up to the present day. He blends the ruins with modern activities: Blaenavon blast furnaces, Telford's great aqueducts, his encounters with large bodies of Methodists. Set beside the ruins, even in Hoare's over-dramatised text, the contrast seems to enhance the perception of both. Tracing the archbishop's route and recalling the reason why he made the journey, the Roman 'stations' either side, ruins of an earlier age, make a powerful image. The picturesque descriptions of the natural background also add to the atmosphere, even if we are not, like Hoare, 'men of taste'!

We cannot of course separate the *Itinerary* from Hoare's more famous work on the Wiltshire prehistoric antiquities as, to some extent, the two overlap. The serial publication of the *Ancient History of Wiltshire* took place between 1810 and 1821. The contrast is astonishing: the wealth of surveyed plans and the fine drawings of pots and other objects found in the barrows. 'Picturesque' has disappeared and the

Figure 8 *Llanthony Priory, drawn by Colt Hoare.*

Figure 9 *Hoare's 'villa' overlooking Lake Bala, drawn by himself.*

23

whole approach is more detached, more scientific. The two-volume work has become the earliest textbook of British prehistory. The evidence used in one case is material and earthworks while with the other, the *Itinerary*, took its very name from a written document. The scheme adopted for Wiltshire of setting up a 'station' from which to make an *iter* out from this at once reminds us of Hoare in Wales.

1805 saw the first part of John Britton's *The Architectural Antiquities of Great Britain, Represented and Illustrated in a Series of Views, Elevations, Plans, Sections and Details of Various Ancient Edifices with Historical and Descriptive Accounts of Each* (first volume 1807). It was a profound change, with complete plans, sections, detail of vaults, mouldings etc. The 'picturesque' as a form of recording just disappeared; it could not compete. Hoare, now on his home ground, simply had to alter his whole treatment even if his work was non-architectural. The quality of drawings, plans and much else had to be improved, although this does not detract from the originality of Hoare's ideas in either of the projects he undertook.

No doubt in the long run *Ancient Wiltshire* had far more influence for it is a more impressive work, and yet there is a fascination about Baldwin's journey and no less about Hoare in Wales. If one promoted the value of earthworks and barrows, the other promoted the value of ruins.

Notes

1   For Colt Hoare and Stourhead see Woodbridge 1970. Hoare 1806 and 1810–2. Woodbridge used the Cardiff MSS but seems to have been unaware that there were two sets of evidently different dates.
2   Nichols 1840.
3   JCH.
4   Wyndham 1775, 1781.
5   Hoare 1806.
6   Pennant 1778–81.
7   Coxe 1801.
8   Fenton 1811.
9   Coxe 1801, vol ii, 228.
10   JCH 186, 188.
11   *ibid*, 42.
12   *ibid*, 226.
13   Woodbridge 1970.
14   Hoare 1806, 411–33. Carter's scheme was cumbersome and difficult to remember.
15   JCH 159–60.
16   *ibid*, 111.
17   *ibid*. Hoare was among the anti-restorers supported by the Society of Antiquaries.
18   *ibid*, 73.
19   *ibid*, 181.
20   *ibid*, 83.
21   *ibid*, 123.
22   *ibid*, 86.
23   *ibid*, 98.
24   *ibid*, 233.
25   *ibid*, 211.
26   *ibid*, 206.
27   *ibid*, 147.
28   *ibid*, 63.
29   *ibid*, 185–6.
30   E Pugh 1816, 283.
31   JCH 62.

32 *ibid,* 67.
33 *ibid,* 68.
34 *ibid,* 35.
35 *ibid,* 239, 243.
36 E Pugh 1816, 283–4.
37 Hoare 1807.
38 Coxe 1801.
39 Hoare 1806.
40 Hoare was associated with John Carter and the Society of Antiquaries in objections to Wyatt's cathedral restorations.

Chapter 3

Conscience and Restoration – Ruskin and Morris

Colt Hoare never mentions God in his diaries, and the Welsh Methodists that he met in North Wales did not cause him to admire their piety but to regard them rather as a curiosity. Although Coxe, with whom he travelled, was a Church of England priest Hoare's religion, if he had any, seems to have been lukewarm. The last ten years of his life (he died in 1838) saw a complete change in the religious atmosphere. Nothing illustrates this better than the last and fifth volume of Britton's *Architectural Antiquities,* which, as we have seen, influenced Hoare's *Ancient Wiltshire:* it suddenly added to its title *A Chronological History and Graphic Illustrations of Christian Architecture in England* (1827). It demonstrates the marriage of Gothic architecture (now datable) with religion to give Christian Architecture. The 'in England' in the title also indicates the patriotic infusion into the subject which became stronger later in the century.

The actual details of the religious revival have been recounted many times, from the Act of 1818 for founding new churches and the founding of Church Building Society, Pugin father and son, the Oxford Movement, which started in 1833, and the architectural societies in Oxford (1839) and Cambridge (1840).[1] From building new churches to rebuilding old ones, introducing High Church liturgies with the alterations that this needed; all required massive 'restoration'. This is perhaps best described by Thomas Hardy in 1906 who, as a young architect, had been engaged in church work soon after the period of the great reconstruction. He wrote:

> 'ctive destruction under saving names has been effected upon so gigantic a scale that the incidental protection of structures or portions of structures, by their being kept wind and waterproof through such operations counts as nothing in the balance. Its enormous magnitude is realised by few...[2]

Many churches by the early nineteenth century were in such a state of neglect as to be ruins (Hoare refers to this at Llandaff cathedral) and so we can, in our story, speak of a large number of ruined or partially ruined churches being restored and brought back into use, even if this was accompanied by the sort of destruction referred to by Hardy. The 'restoration' was not confined to churches but affected many secular buildings, such as the Tower of London, Windsor Castle, Cardiff Castle and so on.

It is not the intention here to praise or condemn this extraordinary outburst of Gothic building activity, nor its most interesting, albeit controversial, aspect, its motivation. It is sufficient here to record its happening, for we are really concerned with the reaction against it, which so profoundly influenced attitudes to Gothic architecture in buildings in use as much as ruined examples.

The 'reaction' against 'restoration' is, of course, associated with John Ruskin (1819–1900), beginning with one of his earliest works, *The Seven Lamps of Architecture* (1849). As a register of the life of a nation:

> All steps are marked most clearly in the arts, and in Architecture more than in any other, for it being specially dependent ... on the warmth of true life is also peculiarly sensible of the hemlock cold of the false.[3]

Ruskin is evidently speaking of 'restoration' and, if I understand him correctly, of the loss of spontaneity in the work, and he refers to the 'craftsman', for it is in terms of crafts that Ruskin is largely thinking. It is the state of mind of the craftsman that is at the heart of Ruskin's thinking: 'For we are not sent into this world to do anything into which we cannot put our hearts.'[4]

The sequence is admiration for Gothic architecture, raised to reverence by its Christian association, then admiration for the craftsmanship which required superb craftsmen. This then became admiration for a society that produced it, contrasted with horrors of modern industrial society. William Morris achieved the extreme form of medieval idyll, causing him to become an active socialist recreating medieval society in modern form in the arts and crafts society. Ruskin hardly passed beyond the third stage.

One begins to understand Ruskin's attitude towards restoration. Age is a building's greatest attribute:

> For indeed, the greatest glory of a building is not in its stones, nor in its gold. Its glory is in its Age…we feel in walls that have long been washed by passing waves of humanity…I think a building cannot be considered as in its prime until four or five centuries have passed over it.[5]

Now for restoration:

> Neither by the public, nor by those who have the care of public monuments is the true meaning of the word *restoration* understood. It means the most total destruction which a building can suffer: a destruction out of which no remnants can be gathered…Do not let us deceive ourselves in this important matter; it is impossible, as impossible to raise the dead to restore anything that has ever been great or beautiful in architecture. Do not let us talk then of restoration. The thing is a lie from beginning to end. We have no right whatever to touch them. They are not ours. They belong partly to those who built them, and partly to all the generations of mankind who are to follow us.[6]

Ruskin put architecture above all other arts:

> Architecture, her continual influence over the emotions of daily life, and her realism, as opposed to the two sister arts which are in comparison but the picturing of stones and of dreams…I say architecture and all art; for I believe architecture must be the beginning of art and those others must follow in their time and order…[7]

Architecture in these quotations means Gothic architecture and, the principal ruins being Gothic, the effect was to raise their status. Ruskin usually uses Continental examples of intact buildings but in his speech on the opening of the Crystal Palace transferred to Sydenham he referred to the ruined Scottish Cistercian abbey of Melrose (Roxburghshire) where he urged '…touch not the actual edifice, except in so far as it may be necessary to sustain, to protect it.'[8]

The original stones themselves were endowed by Ruskin with a virtue of their own as this quotation from an article in *The American Architect and Builder* (1870) by J. H.

Chamberlain referring to a ruined abbey illustrates:

> …The walls may be shattered, the groining of the roof may have fallen, the aisles may be choked with weeds or rendered impassable by rubbish, but where there are even two or three stones left standing one upon the other, the old life and the old glory are abiding with them.[9]

The language is exaggerated but the debt to Ruskin is evident. Ruined abbeys had clearly come into their own!

Ruskin's efforts to mount a campaign against 'restoration' through the Society of Antiquaries did not take off, but his more dramatic gesture, refusal of the Gold Medal of the Royal Institute of British Architects, had a much greater impact on opinion.[10] In his letter of 20 May 1873 to the Secretary 'the destruction under the name of restoration of the most celebrated works for the sake of emolument' was his reason for his refusal. On 12 June he confirmed that members of the RIBA were 'assuredly responsible'. The medal was then awarded to G. E. Street.

Ruskin had no professional qualifications but the man of action who now appears and took over was a qualified architect who had worked under Street. William Morris was more of an arts and crafts man who had had his own business.[11] He and Phillip Webb created the Society for the Protection of Ancient Buildings (SPAB) which held its first meeting on 22 March 1877.

The SPAB held annual meetings, the reports of which will be discussed below. Its membership was widely spread but it had a social cachet with aristocratic and influential membership and so carried quite a lot of punch.[12] Lubbock and Curzon and, as we have seen, Thomas Hardy spoke in it. In its early years its officers were professional with Morris as Secretary.

The first annual report, as expected, lamented the damage done in the previous 50 years. It was to be a 'rallying point' for collecting and expressing a rational interest.[13] There was a right to preserve and repair but not to restore. How many churches had been restored and how many were still intact? Inquiries were set on foot. 'Deplorable falsification has been for long going on to ancient buildings.' Earthworks and monastic buildings would fall within their purview.

In 1879 Professor Bryce justified their work:

> There is no kind of historical evidence which is so precious, so certain, so incontrovertible as that supplied by ancient buildings…and so our ancient buildings present in themselves a complete picture of the taste and skill displayed at any point of time.

From now on it became usual for cases to be listed where the Society had intervened or at all events advised.

At the 1882 meeting Bryce was in the chair and it emerged that the First Commissioner of Works was a member of the Society who 'is so thoroughly imbued with and interested in its principles that he is going to bring in a Bill on the subject'. The First Commissioner then was Rt. Hon. Shaw-Lefevre, later Lord Eversley.

In 1883 the Crown's work at the Tower of London was criticised in an extremely interesting speech by Sir John Lubbock, who explained why the 1882 Act fell short of what he had intended:

> The main principal of our Bill was that where the owner of an ancient monument wished to

destroy it…it was a very modest request that the country should be allowed to purchase and preserve it. To our great surprise that principle was hotly contested by a very few members of the House of Commons on the grounds of its interference with property…

The first mention of a ruin, Kirkstall Abbey, came up and continued the next and following years. The Society had few remedies to suggest except waterproofing. It emerged that the main adversaries of the Society were the 'priesthood'!

In 1884 Morris astonished the Society by giving his major speech advocating socialism.[14] In 1887 we learned that 'architects as a body', including surveyors, are 'most strongly opposed to the Society'. It took a long time for the views of Morris to be generally adopted, only indeed by the early years of the next century.

By 1895 ruins were featuring regularly in the report and owners were offered advice: as at Hadleigh Castle, Essex; Jewry Wall, Leicester; John of Gaunt's Hall at Lincoln; and Worksop Abbey gatehouse.

In 1902, in their 25th Report, the Society was able to congratulate themselves that the uphill task they had set themselves in 1877, when 'restoration' was in full swing, to persuade architects to desist had been achieved but:

> Much was done to disabuse the mind…that the Society would rather see ancient buildings fall to ruin than that they should be repaired…the efforts made have generally borne fruit.[15]

So, at the time when serious legislation for protecting ruins was being mooted, this battle had been largely (but by no means entirely) won and this would be taken on board by the Office of Works when they started the retrieval and repair of ruins.

In 1903 the SPAB issued *Notes on the Repair of Ancient Buildings*:

> But unfortunately the wish to make the buildings perfect, the desire to have everything complete, gave rise to the craze for restoration so called, the effect of which has been to make many ancient buildings which were once full of vitality and interest mere modern copies which whether as works of art or as records of the past, are of little value…The restorer is in reality committing a forgery…he falsifies an historical record.[16]

The distinctive feature of SPAB work, the filling of voids with tiers of tiles after decayed stone had been removed, is described. This course of action was not adopted by the Office of Works which, for this as in many other matters, had a much more flexible approach. The *Notes* are not very helpful on ruins, merely advocating the removal of ivy and waterproofing.

* * * * *

The views of Ruskin had by about 1900 been very widely adopted over much of Europe but in France in the mid nineteenth century very different views were held, particularly associated with E. Viollet-le-Duc, famous for his restorations. Fortunately, in his great *Dictionnaire*, he has an article entitled *Restoration* (Appendix 1), the opening lines of which give us a good idea of how he thought on this subject:

> The word and the thing are modern. To restore a building is not to maintain it, not to repair it, not to renovate it, it is to re-establish it in a finished state that can never have existed at any given moment.[17]

He goes on to explain that it could not have been done before because the level of knowledge of past architecture did not allow it. It was a kind of Platonic ideal that he had in mind, made possible by advances in knowledge. It was the very antithesis of Ruskin's view.

It was of course a theory specifically applicable to ruins and it is in Viollet-le-Duc's restorations at Carcassone and Pierrefonds that the theory was put into practice. However, we do not need to cross the Channel to see work in Viollet-le-Duc's style, for at Castell Coch (Red Castle), just north of Cardiff, William Burges did just such a restoration on a very fragmentary thirteenth-century castle ruin for the second Marquess of Bute.[18] The Marquess was a Roman Catholic convert and besides the restoration of the castle there was to be a vineyard (later well known for its wines), creating the atmosphere around a French chateau. Burges designed not only the building but also the furniture and decorations inside.

In 1875 Burges produced a volume with plans and sections of the castle before restoration and proposals for the work (Figure 10). Although a small castle was chosen for the experiment, the main reason for its completion and success, a massive clearance operation had already taken place, clearing great quantities of debris from the encircling ditch and in the courtyard. One can see how much of the castle had to be rebuilt: the ground plan presented no problems but the towers, internal rooms, curtain wall, roofs etc had to be 'restored'. Accurate 'restoration' is virtually a contradiction in terms but Burges certainly made a very impressive job, being as close as he could. He tried to justify his pepper-pot roofs on the towers, which might have been possible for a thirteenth-century French castle but seem out of place in Wales! The original masonry in the lower part is distinguishable from the work of Burges. One must admire the skill with which this handsome 'restoration' was carried out.

The castle is much sought after by television companies and is fairly popular with the public. It has a modern 'portcullis' and modern drawbridge that can be operated. The visual impact is of course much more attractive than a ruin treated as found: the general public far prefers a 'restoration' or folly than a Ruskinesque ruin. The total reconstruction of the *Principia* of the Roman Limes fort of Saalburg (also set in attractive woodland) done 100 years ago at the orders of the Kaiser, which attracts a quarter of million visitors a year, is another example of the popularity of such 'restorations'.[19]

In both cases the low remains gave the restorers a much freer hand and allowed a clear distinction to be made between what was there already and the modern creation. In one case the very considerable costs were met privately by the Marquess and in the other presumably came from official sources. Cost is the central issue in the discussion. Furthermore, as the number of traditional craftsmen dwindles and modern building techniques diverge more and more from traditional ones, so the difficulties increase. The matter will come up again.

Enough has been said to bring out the fundamental difference in attitudes towards ruins in England and in France in the nineteenth century. In the former, religion was at first the overriding consideration, turning gradually into a matter of conscience, while in France religion played little part, following instead the relentless logic of Viollet-le-Duc.

* * * * *

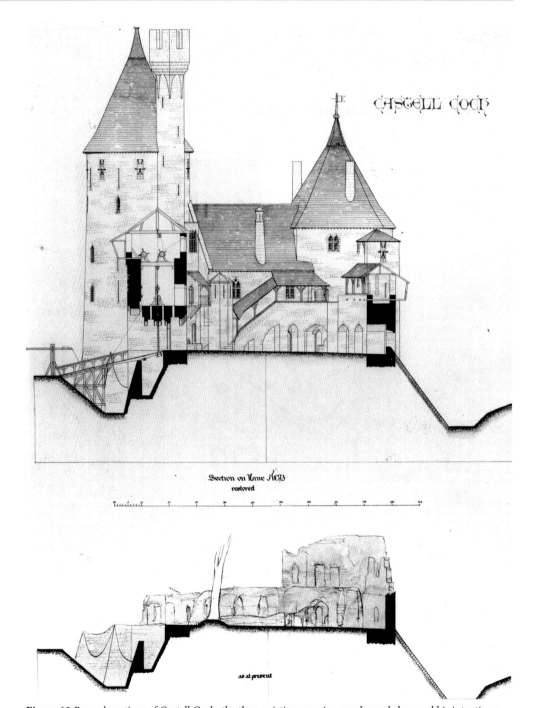

CASTELL COCH

Section on line AEB
restored

as at present

Figure 10 *Burges's sections of Castell Coch: the then-existing remains are shown below and his intentions above.*

Figure 11 *Aerial view of Castel Coch as 'restored' by Burges.*

While voluntary bodies, for obvious reasons, had little to do with ruins in the nineteenth century we cannot pass over in silence the work of the National Trust, founded in 1894.[20] It had grown from the Commons Preservation Society (CPS) ,founded in 1866 with the very worthy purpose and object of preserving the common land of the country. Its connection with ancient monuments was accidental since ruins or earthworks might occur on the commons in question, which might promote their survival. The extension of ownership by landowners, which is what was resisted, might be a real threat to a monument. Some of the people involved, such as Robert Hunter, who played a leading part in defence of the commoners, certainly saw the matter in terms of conscience.

Octavia Hill, with a background of Nonconformist philanthropy, enjoyed a long association with John Ruskin. She became involved with the CPS through her work on retaining open spaces in towns. She was a stout opponent of the legislation that facilitated enclosure of commons and so was drawn into the CPS. She published an article promising the benefits to working people of Lubbock's Bank Holiday Act, which allowed them time to visit the countryside. The overlapping of interests is plain. The last of the famous trio of the Trust founders was Canon Hardwicke Rawnsley, from Cumbria.

Hitherto the agitation had been in the Courts or Parliament and it was only the decision to create a body that could hold property that brought the National Trust into being. Its inaugural meeting was held on 16 July 1894. It was primarily concerned with scenery but inevitably an estate might contain buildings or ruins. Two major examples of ruins later came into the hands of the Trust, Bodiam and Tattershall castles. After spending large sums on retrieval and treatment Lord Curzon bequeathed them to the Trust. Ruins were hardly its forte until the recent interest in rural industrial machinery such as mills, beam engines and so on. Some of these might be regarded as features in areas of natural beauty, in the preservation of which the Trust has always been active.

Over the years, the Trust has been caught up in a social revolution that has caused many impoverished, often aristocratic, landowners to place their great country houses (with an endowment) in its hands. At the same time the universal motorcar has made even the remotest of such houses accessible to the public. So a happy solution has been reached by which the Trust at its own charge displays roofed and furnished houses while the Ministry of Works (now English Heritage) maintains and displays the non-commercial ruins as a charge on public funds.

* * * * *

Before turning to Ireland, it may be useful to refer, briefly, to the advances in the study of medieval architecture in the nineteenth century, a subject worthy of a book in its own right, since the remains we are principally concerned with are medieval. The advances were mainly in ecclesiastical architecture with the secular side following behind. Understanding the existing buildings is basic to understanding the fragmentary ruins, usually only part of a larger building or group of buildings.

The nomenclature for the periods, worked out by Thomas Rickman in 1817,[21] had not been used as a tool for studying the architectural history of a building until Robert Willis (1800–75) did so, brilliantly, at the meeting of the British Archaeological Association at Canterbury Cathedral in 1845.[22] He followed it with similar studies on other cathedrals, bringing the documentary and architectural evidence into close association. In later life he made even more detailed studies combining the two sources in his posthumous work *The Architectural History of the University of Cambridge and the Colleges of Cambridge and Eton,* published by his nephew in 1886. Willis, a Professor of Engineering at Cambridge, introduced a serious, scientific and down-to-earth approach to the whole subject (in contrast to Ruskin and Morris), and dominated medieval architectural studies in the latter half of the nineteenth century and, to great extent, ever since.

At the end of the nineteenth century a new element came into the subject, completing the dated plan (the object of the exercise) by excavation that was very crude by today's standards, but still quite effective. The coloured dated plan is one of the distinctive features of reports in the journals before the First World War. The chief exponent of such work was William St John Hope (1854–1919), then Assistant Secretary of the Society of Antiquaries, who worked on abbeys and castles (Ludlow and Windsor).[23] Unfortunately his plans are too large to reproduce in this book.

Our knowledge of ruins advanced out of all recognition, first through the far better understanding of intact buildings from the historical approach of Willis while, in cases of ruins where guardianship was contemplated, the information as to how the fragmentary ruins then fitted into the general plan was of incalculable value. Indeed the dated plan has become the *sine qua non* of monuments in care and their guidebooks. It is a matter of common sense that a full ground plan of a ruin can be produced even if the elevations may always elude us (see Figure 23).

* * * * *

In the last section of this chapter I want to turn our view to Ireland, which in the nineteenth century, after the Act of Union,[24] became part of the United Kingdom. Our attention tends to concentrate on political events like the Famine, the Land Problem and Home Rule but there was in fact much that happened which is highly relevant to our subject and which deserves discussion.

The first matter that attracts attention is the subject of maps: that is, large-scale maps, the old Ordnance Survey maps at a scale of 6 inches and 25 inches to the mile. The part played by these in all fieldwork or excavation is fundamental not only to any serious preservation work but also to all field archaeology. The mapping of Britain by the Ordnance Survey had started in 1791 but maps produced at one inch to the mile are too small to properly locate, let alone survey, the site of antiquities – neither ruins nor accidental finds such as coin hoards. The 6-inch and 25-inch maps show field and property divisions and the notice of scheduling has a photocopy of the relevant part of such a map attached showing the 'scheduled area'. In Ireland the survey for 6-inch coverage had started in the 1820s[25] and was completed by 1846, about 40 years before it was done in England.

The matter has a special interest in that Pitt-Rivers (then Colonel Lane-Fox) was stationed in Cork in the 1860s and so the 6-inch maps were available to him; he no doubt made use of them when counting the raths in Munster for they saved a lot of footwork.[26] Indeed his introduction to excavation that culminated so dramatically in Sussex and Cranborne Chase may well owe something to Irish large-scale maps.

The dramatic change for ruins specifically came with the Irish Church Act of 1869 and the disestablishment of the Church of Ireland, caused by the fact that the majority of the population were Roman Catholics and so did not belong to the established church. Section 25 of the Act provided for the preservation of ruinous or wholly unused structures 'deserving of being maintained as a national monument', being vested in the Secretary of the Commissioners of Public Works 'to be preserved as a national monument'.[27] There was no provision in Britain for the care of the ancient monuments until 1882 so, as Wheeler says: 'In this matter, as in the provision of a detailed map of the country on the 6 inch scale Ireland was actually in the lead'.[28]

The Board of Works received its first monument, 'the ruins of the Ancient Cathedral Church on the Rock of Cashel', in October 1874, and in December thirteen more were 'vested': Devenish, Donaghmore (County Tyrone), Monasterboice, Donaghmore (County Meath), St Columbs House, Kells, the Round Tower of Killation, Kilkierran and Alenny, antiquities at Ardmore, Glendalough and Ardert and last, but not least, Gallarus Oratory.[29] These include some of the most well-known Irish monuments.

The man in charge, Thomas Deane, the Superintendent, as he was then called, and subsequently Inspector, took charge in March 1875 'which may be taken as the effective beginning of the Board's involvement in National Monuments'.[30] By 1875 there were 105 'vested' monuments, a number that increased in time. Wheeler, upon whose work this information is based, quotes a paragraph from the Board's Report of 1875–6:

The Instructions which the Board have given to their Architect and to the Superintendent who has been appointed to take immediate charge of the ruins, are that their operations are to be strictly confined to what is necessary for the preservation of several monuments– securing loose stones, preventing infiltration of water by cement covering the walls etc where practicable, and clearing away rubbish, where, by doing so portions of the buildings now hidden may, with advantage, be brought to view but carefully to avoid any attempt at restoration, or doing anything which might mar the ancient and picturesque character of the ruins.[31]

It will be noticed that there is to be *no restoration*, although it appears that some did take place on the remoter sites where Deane could not go.

In 1882 the Ancient Monuments Protection Act, which applied to Britain and Ireland, the only legislation of this kind ever to do so, came into force. It will be discussed in the next chapter but what strikes one immediately is the contrast between ruins 'vested' in the Irish Board of Works and the earthworks, stone circles, cairns etc in the 'Schedule' at the end of the Act (See Appendix 3). The point is that the Board was spending money (£50,000) on preservation while the object of the Act was to confine its operation to monuments that preserved themselves without significant cost. The Superintendent in Ireland changed his title to Inspector (statutorily authorised), while in Britain the Inspector (Pitt-Rivers) was clearly no architect and never had to confront real large ruins.

Sir John Lubbock, the author of *Prehistoric Times* (first edition 1865) was particularly interested in preserving the evidence for the antiquity of man and so in his own Bill he confined his attention to field monuments, not large ruins.[32] When the new Government took on the Bill, which had been private, obviously it found cost-free preservation attractive. In the debates, Lubbock had been accused of furthering his own interests by leaving out the religious ruins in which most people were interested. The matter can be pursued in the next chapter.

Notes

1   Thompson 1990; Piggott 1976, 101–133, 171–97.
2   Hardy 1906.
3   Ruskin 1849, 156–7.
4   *ibid*, 182.
5   *ibid*, 195 and 202.
6   *ibid*, 205 and 206.
7   *ibid*, 211 and 215.
8   Ruskin, *Collected Works*, Vol 12, 433.
9   Quoted in Brooks 1987, 73.
10 Harris 1963.
11 MacCarthy 1994, 375–78.
12 The *Annual Reports of SPAB* meetings list the members.
13 Where I am referring to *Annual reports of SPAB* I will not give a reference within them.
14 MacCarthy 1994, 464–86, 494, 508–9, 655–6. Morris read *Das Kapital* in a French version in 1880 and subsequently became an active 'revolutionary' socialist in the democratic Federation in which Marx's daughter, Eleanor, was a leading member.
15 SPAB *Annual report*, 1902, 16.
16 SPAB 1903.
17 A shortened version of Viollet-le-Duc's article in the *Dictionnaire* can be found in Appendix 1.
18 A full account of Burges's proposals by himself was lent to the Welsh Office, which is now returned to Mount Stuart Library, Bute. Figure 10 is based on this.

19   Ulbert and Weber 1985.
20   Fedden 1967, Murphy 1987.
21   Thomas Rickman, architect (1774–1841), *DNB*.
22   Thompson 1996, also *DNB*. Robert Willis (1800–1875) was elected Jacksonian Professor of Applied Mechanics in 1837. Although author of numerous archaeological articles in his lifetimes his only book was *Principles of Mechanism,* 1841 and second edition 1870.
23   Hope's publications, largely on abbeys, are listed in A.H. Thompson 1929.
24   Sir Howard Colvin has drawn my attention to a cognate responsibility of the short-lasting Scottish Works Office (1821–39) for redundant cathedrals, two abbeys, Scottish Exchequer and Holyrood House palace, which were partly ruinous (Colvin, *History of the King's Works,* vi, 251–54). The abolition of the Scottish episcopacy meant that cathedrals were no longer cathedrals.
25   Andrews 1975, especially 127–29. The early 6-inch sheets are handsomely produced, with the circular early medieval raths sprinkled over them, especially in the Cork area.
26   Thompson 1977, 45–6.
27   Wheeler 1975.
28   *ibid.*
29   *ibid*, 81.
30   *ibid.*
31   *ibid*, 82.
32   Kains-Jackson 1880. In his long preface Lubbock explained his own classification system for prehistoric monuments and his omission of any other kind of monument leaves little doubt about his interests.

Chapter 4

Science – Lubbock and Pitt-Rivers

We move now into an entirely different field, where the ruins have no contemporary records, coming as they do when writing was either unknown or only known a long way away. All that we know of their creators has to be derived from the surviving remains and comparison of these with similar ones elsewhere. This type of monument only became properly understood once it was appreciated that the period of written records is only the tail-end of a vastly longer period of time, during which the presence of man can be inferred from the material remains and interference in the landscape that he left behind. This happened quite abruptly when, in 1859, Joseph Prestwich and John Evans visited the Somme valley and confirmed that the flint tools found by Boucher de Perthes in the gravels were associated with the bones of extinct animals and so of great antiquity.[1] The well-known lecture that they gave to the Royal Society after their visit is normally regarded as the starting point for the general acceptance of the antiquity of man. The man who, to his regret, was not present in the famous visit, who popularised this and other discoveries, was Sir John Lubbock (1834–1913), later Lord Avebury, taking his title from the great prehistoric temple in Wiltshire. It is to him that attention must now be turned.

Lubbock lived from childhood to his death at Down, Kent, the village to which Charles Darwin came while Lubbock was still a small boy. Unhappy at Eton, Lubbock left there at 14, joining his father's bank at 15. From then onwards, his main means of livelihood were from banking, which yielded a very substantial income. Natural history was his particular interest, in which he was guided or taught by Darwin himself (Appendix 2). He had a distinguished career in this and was, needless to say, at the forefront of the Theory of Evolution, although his studies in biology need not detain us.[2] Archaeology and anthropology became special interests and he visited Scandinavia, Swiss lake villages and the Dordogne in pursuit of this. In 1865 he published *Prehistoric Times as illustrated by Ancient Remains and the Manners and Customs of Modern Savages* (seventh edition 1913). It was written in a simple and lucid style, which explains the frequent issue of new editions. He invented the terms Palaeolithic, Neolithic, Bronze Age and Iron Age, that we still use today. Running into almost as many editions was his *The Origin of Civilisation and the Primitive Condition of Man* (1870). This was ethnographic in its treatment and for that reason worldwide in its application. The point is that he had virtually created prehistoric archaeology as a subject in popular books even before he entered Parliament in 1870.

He undertook many public duties and a political career from 1870 onwards. Soon after he entered the Commons, he introduced a Private Bill that became the Bank Holiday Act. The introduction of the August Bank Holiday was immensely popular and so strengthened his position although, being in opposition, he held no Government office. This was the basis on which, from 1873, he set out for the rest of the decade to push his Ancient Monuments Bill through Parliament.

Now we must turn to the other player, Augustus Pitt-Rivers. Like Lubbock, he had no university education although he was at Sandhurst for a period; his was a military career that took him to the Crimea, Malta, Canada and, as discussed above (p.34), Ireland.[3] As with Lubbock or John Evans, archaeology was a hobby and not his livelihood. He started as a collector at the time of the Great Exhibition, not just collecting any particular type of object but, rather, a sequence of objects intended to illustrate the development of a certain tool or weapon. It was a sort of universal typology, not a Bronze Age typology of the type associated with Montelius. He relied mainly on ethnographic material and believed that if he could obtain a full sample, all the series would run back to a few initial examples, as evolution had demonstrated in the biological world. We cannot discuss the theory here but it did not deter Darwin from signing his proposal form for the Royal Society.[4] To his collecting interests he added fieldwork in Ireland and, perhaps through Christy, the excavator of French caves, he became a prehistorian and collector of archaeological material. In the 1870s, now as a well-known prehistorian, he was making very successful excavations on the Sussex hillforts.[5]

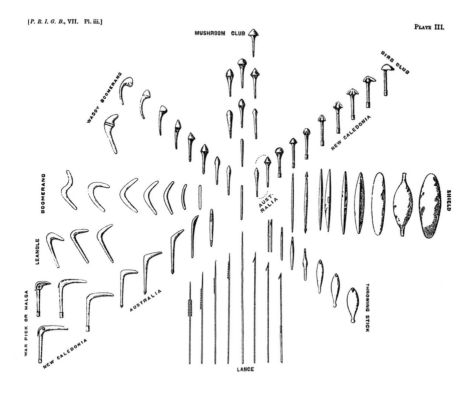

Figure 12 *Diagram by Pitt-Rivers to show development ('evolution') of primitive weapons*

At what point he came into close association with Lubbock is not clear, but he was named as one of the seven special Commissioners who, together with the nominated ones, were to oversee the implementation of Lubbock's Bill if it became an Act. The list of monuments attached to the 1882 Act was largely comprised of prehistoric sites, exclusively in England and Wales, and it is not impossible that Pitt-Rivers had helped in the selection. Although the two men were temperamentally very different, they evidently had in common a belief in the importance of the discoveries about early man then being made. It was the struggles of Lubbock from 1873 onwards (only a first reading of his Bill in that year) that brought them together. They belonged to numerous societies where they could have met to discuss the Bill and, while it cannot be proven, there seems little doubt that in Lubbock's view Pitt-Rivers held a special position on the project.

An essential element in the operation of the Bill, if and when it became law, was for an individual to be able to confront private owners on the proposed restriction of their rights – not always a particularly pleasant task. Colonel Lane-Fox, with senior military rank and accustomed to authority, apart from his 'county' background, might well be considered the right man. In 1878–9, the Bill had achieved a second reading and even encouragement from the Government, who recommended changing the nominated Commissioners to the Trustees of the British Museum. There was a group of determined opponents and so, finally, it was referred to a Select Committee in the absence of Lubbock, with the knowledge that the impending dissolution of Parliament would kill it.[6] Lubbock lost his Maidstone seat at the election but soon returned, sitting for London University. In due course a Government Bill, an emasculated form of Lubbock's, became the 1882 Act.

Pitt-Rivers could not foresee this in 1878–9, when his duties as Commissioner-designate might still be needed. The hillforts of Sussex were utterly different from the predominantly megalithic monuments in the England and Wales part of the Schedule to the Bill and what better preparation than to go to the Mecca of megalithic studies, Brittany? There would be no suspicion of jumping the gun; he even deceived his modern biographer who thought his Breton visits in October/November 1878 and March/April 1879 were pure coincidence![7]

I have described the two notebooks covering these visits and it need not be repeated here.[8] The objects drawn or surveyed were by no means exclusively megalithic, particularly in 1879, but the plan and elevation of, for example, the gallery grave at Pleudihan can leave little doubt that megaliths were his main interest. He started off in 1878 in the classic megalithic area of the Morbihan.

The families of Pitt-Rivers and Lubbock were linked in 1884 when Lubbock married Alice, the daughter of Pitt-Rivers, after the death of his first wife.[9] The fortunes of Lane-Fox had, meanwhile, changed out of all recognition when he inherited the 20,000 acre estate of Cranborne Chase overlapping Dorset, Hampshire and Wiltshire. Part of the condition of the bequest was that he changed his name to Pitt-Rivers.[10] We will have to return to his new-found wealth, or rather how he used it, later but first we must examine his new title of 'Inspector of Ancient Monuments'.

All the circumstances of 'The making of the First Ancient Monuments Act, 1882' have been studied in great detail by Chippendale,[11] while I have described the journeys

Figure 13 *Pitt-Rivers acting as scale by a standing stone at Shap, drawn by Tomkin.*

of the Inspector[12] from the notebooks carried on those journeys and given by his eldest son to the Office of Works, now in the National Archve. It would be tedious to describe all this detail here as the interested reader can consult the references given there.

Both Lubbock's private Bill and the Government's Act of 1882 concluded with a schedule or list of monuments to which they applied, divided among England and Wales, Scotland and Ireland. We can omit the last which came under Dublin (see pp.34–5). Lubbock's schedule, however, had 38 monuments in England and Wales and 19 in Scotland, while the Act had 29 in the one, 21 in the other, a slight reduction from 57 to 50. They were entirely prehistoric in England, megalithic predominantly, while in Scotland they were predominantly prehistoric with some medieval. Lubbock, in his preface to Kains-Jackson's *Our Ancient Monuments* (1880), was clearly thinking in exclusively prehistoric terms, but in fact the criterion was that there were no maintenance costs other than fencing. Additions to the Schedule could be and were made by the cumbersome process of Order in Council.

What was done by the Office of Works to protect the monuments in the Schedule? In Lubbock's Bill, in the event of the owner wishing to alter or destroy the monument, he had first to offer it for sale to the Government, but in the Act the 'registration' of the monument was purely voluntary, and until it was registered, a form of guardianship, it was afforded no protection whatsoever. About half the owners refused to enter into such an agreement and so were not affected by the Act. Its permissive character, therefore, made the Act a very feeble instrument. No measures for preservation are really workable unless there is some degree of compulsion behind the velvet glove. Both Bill and Act fell down on the 'museum attitude' of ownership or in the limited form of guardianship, which was seen as the only solution. The simple designation of the monument as an ancient monument, the *monument historique* of Choay, requiring compulsory notice of intention to alter or destroy with penalties for failure to do so, was the proper solution that was only introduced in 1913.

Lubbock's Bill, had it become law, probably envisaged executive operations by one

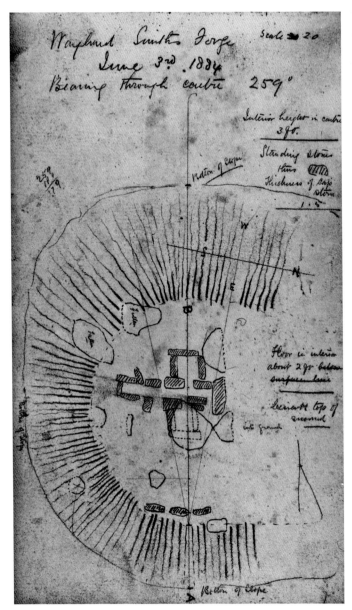

Figure 14 *Plan of Wayland Smithy chambered tomb, by Tomkin, accompanying Pitt-Rivers on an Inspection tour.*

or more of the seven special Commissioners referred to above. The Government had suggested that the Commission be replaced by the Trustees of the British Museum, which would have given a decidedly museum aspect to the organisation, but would no doubt have been more compliant than the quango proposed by Lubbock. The executive arm would have been a Keeper in the Bloomsbury style!

It never happened because of the failure of the Bill. Therefore, under the Government Act, the organisation could have been redesigned to fit the Office of Works mould with an Inspector in charge, such as the Dublin Superintendent, and modelled on inspectors in education and elsewhere. When offered the post on which Lubbock had chivvied the 'First Commissioner', Pitt-Rivers, was concerned about its status –as well he might be.

The post of Inspector, being part time with a salary of £250 per annum, not so grand as the post of Commissioner, was given up by Pitt-Rivers in 1890. He probably saw it in grander terms harking back to Lubbock's Commission. In actual fact, it really was a very happy solution since it was not so demanding as to interfere with the great excavations in Cranborne Chase, and at the same time threw a cloak of officialdom over them, even if they were entirely self-financed. A Lieutenant-General with a lifetime of loyal service did expect official recognition of his activities, especially when the results of this work were published in such sumptuous form.

One advantage of being within a Government department such as the Office of Works was the availability of support staff that could carry out routine work such as dealing with correspondence. From 1883 Pitt-Rivers undertook annual journeys visiting monuments named in the Schedule or others that interested him or were offered in guardianship by owners. The field notebooks that he carried with him in England, Wales and Scotland have survived and a summary account of them has been published.[13] He normally travelled with two or three assistants, partly to handle the bulky equipment and help in the recording and surveying. From 1880, his newly found wealth allowed him to employ four or five assistants, who took charge of the excavations and carried out museum and other activities, including accompanying the General on his journeys. They did much of the recording, which meant drawing and surveying, for it was only in 1888 that a plate camera was bought. The last of the *Excavations in Cranborne Chase* volumes contains many photographic plates, before which all illustrations were drawn by hand.

Figure 15 *Excavation by Pitt-Rivers of Wor Barrow in 1893–4*

In 1883 the readily accessible monuments were dealt with, such as Kit's Coty House megalith in Kent and West Kennet long barrow. In August and September Pitt-Rivers, travelling alone, went up to Scotland and visited the Lake District on the way. The early journeys were very much megalithic journeys in England and Wales, but less so in Scotland, and it was a type of monument for which the owners appear to have been fairly co-operative. He seems to have tried to see individual owners and present them with a copy of the 1882 Act from the supply he carried with him. In 1884 he was in the Midlands, Wales and Scotland, going as far as the Shetlands. In 1885 he reached eastern Scotland and the notebook has fine drawings by Tomkin, perhaps his most talented illustrator among the assistants. In 1886 and 1887 he was again in Scotland, although there is no special notebook for the former year. In 1889, he visited the Cotswolds and South Wales. The next year there were trips by the assistants without the General, and the books then stop. The post now became honorary until his death in 1900 but he had, in fact, done probably as much as the Act made possible by 1890. Also, his health was deteriorating; he suffered from diabetes.

What then had been achieved? According to Chippendale's figures,[14] 24 out 50 monuments in the Schedule had been 'registered', brought into guardianship, together with another 18 monuments offered by the owners. There had been 26 refusals to 'register', slightly more than half of those on the Schedule. These enjoyed no kind of protection. It is a poor showing in relation to the labour involved. The weakness of the Act was the need to accession the monuments in museum fashion, and not outright designation with notice required of alteration or destruction, in effect declaring the remains a 'monument historique' in Choay style.[15] A voluntary method of protection is unworkable since the real threat to monuments is likely to come from the non-volunteers. The nettle was only grasped, and then only hesitantly, in 1913.

What, if anything, was achieved by the 1882 Act and Pitt-Rivers? It is often regarded as a foolish distraction from preserving masonry structures and particularly medieval remains. After the death of Pitt-Rivers, the statutory post went into abeyance for ten years and, when a reappointment was made, the new Inspector was an architect, not an archaeologist. An administrative officer, named Fitzgerald, took charge from 1900 to 1910 and the whole drift of interest in Ancient Monuments tended towards later remains.

A permissive Act was no doubt ineffective, but it was a declaration of principle, a statement of Government responsibility that could not be expunged but might be expanded and built upon. More to the point it showed that preservation was not merely confined to monastic remains but embraced the periods before written records, preserving the record of the whole period of man's presence on the earth, knowledge of which had so dramatically increased in the middle of the nineteenth century. There is something peculiarly satisfying that the first steps in monument preservation in this country should celebrate the discovery of the antiquity of man.

To return to more prosaic matters, how far were the great works of excavation embodied in the four magnificent volumes of *Excavations in Cranborne Chase*, privately printed by Pitt-Rivers, influential in the subsequent development of preservation? With regard to archaeology generally there is no doubt their influence was profound: that by skilful excavation you can date and vastly expand our knowledge of long barrows like Wor Barrow, or linear earthworks like Bokerley Dyke, or native Romano-British sites like Woodcutts and Rotherly. It was not merely techniques of digging that were demonstrated but the very nature of the earthworks, which, properly studied, were in some respects as revealing of the past as masonry remains associated with written records. Lubbock's inclusion of earthworks, i.e. hillforts, in his Schedule was amply vindicated. Treating earthworks as significant works of man was fully justified; the status of earthworks as ruins, the most frequently 'scheduled' monuments, was greatly raised.

Pitt-Rivers and, perhaps to a lesser extent, Lubbock were conscious of the educational value of ruins, prehistoric ones especially. At the beginning of his military career Pitt-Rivers had been involved in the teaching of the use of the rifle as opposed to the smooth-bore musket and wrote a manual on the subject that included topics such as the increased range and the judging of distance.[16] He had a feeling for teaching. Not surprisingly the whole elaborate organisation at Cranborne Chase had a very marked 'presentation' element.[17] At first people had to be enticed to come to this remote area with the Larmer Pleasure Grounds and its theatre, the band, cycle races and so on. The climax of the visit was educational, that is, the Farnham Museum. This was based on the reconstruction of a 'gypsy school', an earlier voluntary school which Pitt-Rivers tried to revive but which did not attract pupils and could not really compete with the compulsory state system being introduced. It was converted into a museum and then redesigned as a purpose-built museum. It was lit from the roof, with display cases on both sides and tables down the middle to support over a hundred models of excavations carried out by the General. These were envisaged, presumably, not so much as a permanent record but as an educational aid, rather like an army sand table. Much of what puzzles us in the Cranborne Chase arrangements had an educational element behind it.

Behind the events of the Lubbock and Pitt-Rivers episode were two men who believed that science could provide a new vision of our past from the study of the surviving physical remains, particularly from the structures which have no written records.

Notes

1   Prestwich 1859.

2   In Appendix 2 the evidence derived from Darwin's letters in the recently published *Correspondence* (Burkhardt and Matt 1985) has been used. Lubbock must have been familiar with Darwin's ideas from his teens; on Natural Selection, Darwin described Lubbock as an 'enthusiastic convert'. See also Hutchinson 1914 and Duff 1934.

3   Thompson 1977. His collections may have been started at the time of the Great Exhibition but his experiences in Ireland seem to have been the turning point as far as archaeology is concerned.

4   The Librarian of the Royal Society very kindly supplied me with a photocopy of the candidature certificate of Pitt-Rivers (Lane-Fox).

5   Thompson 1977, 53ff.

6   The objections to the Bill, which led to its referral to a Select Committee on 26 May 1880 – (*PD (C)* 252, col. 479–87) with the intention to kill it, can best be seen in the debates 14 April 1875 (*PD (C)* 223, col. 879–917); 7 March 1877 (*PD (C)* 234, col. 1527–63); 16 February 1880 (*PD (C)* 250, col. 773–776). It was very much an alliance of landowners who objected primarily to the compulsory powers in the Bill.

7   Bowden 1991, 86–7.

8   Thompson 1977, 61; Thompson 1960.
9   Bowden 1991, family tree on p.4.
10 Thompson 1977, 75ff.
11 Chippendale 1983.
12 Thompson 1960.
13 Thompson, 1960.
14 Chippendale 1983.
15 Choay 2000.
16 See bibliography of Pitt-Rivers in volume 5 of *Cranborne Chase*. A slim *Treatise on Musketry* by Major Lane-Fox (undated but *c*.1850) has survived.
17 Thompson 1977, 79 ff: Thompson and Renfrew 1999. The building has been converted into private housing.

Chapter 5

Imperial Responsibilities – Lord Curzon

At the beginning of the twentieth century Baldwin Brown, a well-known student of early Christian antiquities, published a book on *The Care of Ancient Monuments* (1905). It is largely a list of legislation in the various countries of Europe, almost indeed as if we were talking of football teams: a new element of nationalism had entered the field of ancient monuments which provided a powerful motivation for their protection. The ruin or monument represented the high level of culture of the people then living in the area occupied by the modern nation, often of fairly modern creation. It may be General de Gaulle referring to French cathedrals or even the relative importance of the cave paintings of France or Spain. The nation's heritage is revered for reasons of patriotism. One thinks of the damage inflicted in the First World War by the Germans in the occupied parts of France, more particularly the use of explosives to destroy the great keep at Coucy, which still rankles.[1] This patriotism, identifying with monuments, is relatively modern and its adoption as part of the 'identity' of a modern nation is not very old. If it has helped to loosen the purse strings of Government in forms of protection then it is surely not to be condemned. Part of Lubbock's difficulties was that the climate of opinion did not allow him to invoke patriotism to preserve prehistoric monuments. Today, patriotism has to some degree waned and we have to rely on television or the other wiles of populism to stir popular lethargy towards the monuments out of its customary repose.

Indirectly related to nationalism or, in the case of Britain, to imperialism are the two great listing projects of the turn of the nineteenth century based on county inventories, the one historical and the other architectural. Neither completed the task before them; one has now been wound up and the other is very much out of breath. Both, however, still remain invaluable tools of reference in the areas covered.

The *Victoria History of the Counties of England* (VCH) was first conceived at the Diamond Jubilee of Queen Victoria in 1897, who graciously allowed her name to be given to the project. The first volume was published in 1900, just before the Queen's death. Plagued by financial problems, going completely bankrupt at one period, its adoption by the Institute of Historical Research of London University in 1932 has given it a reasonably secure position.[2] Originally conceived as comprising 160 volumes for the whole country, like most projects of this kind the estimates have grown constantly and now, with the unfinished counties, several hundred volumes must be envisaged. Most counties already had histories, not always complete and of varying degrees of thoroughness, but only in the case of Northumberland does the previous record seem to have been deemed sufficient not to require treatment in the series. Only a proportion of the counties have been completed and sometimes only a single volume has been published, as in the case of Lincolnshire.[3]

From the beginning there were to be two very distinct parts, the introductory sections and the topographical section. The introductory sections were to cover Natural History, the history of the prehistoric, Roman and Anglo-Saxon periods, monastic and political history, etc, although not all these were achieved. The topographical section, divided into hundreds or wapentakes and treated by parishes within these, proved the most difficult section but obviously, from a reference point of view, it was the most important part.

From the point of view of earthworks and ruins the section on earthworks in the introduction and the architectural section would have been valuable had they been written. In point of fact, architectural information is mainly in the topographical section and describes the parish churches, manor houses and so on, normally describing intact and ruinous structures. It is an interesting comment on the views of historians that, even in 1900, it should have been regarded as desirable to help history with a record of surviving material remains. The happy marriage of the two is one of the successes of the Victoria County Histories.

If the author may be permitted to cite an example of the use of the *VCH* it may illustrate this point.[4] In 1954 the author carried out a 'rescue' excavation at Huttons Ambo, near Malton, Yorkshire, on an earthwork overlooking the River Derwent. It soon became apparent that we were dealing with a fortified manor house of the twelfth century, the dating being dependent on the very crude pottery. However, the history in the *VCH* North Riding volume clearly suggested that a certain Colswain, who held the manor by serjeanty of keeping the gate of the king's castle at York, was also likely to have created the fortified manor house. The combination of the sources made the nature of the site more intelligible and seemed to associate its origin with a specific person.

It is of interest that (later Sir) Charles Peers, appointed to fill the post of Inspector after the interregnum of 10 years following the death of Pitt-Rivers, was an architect (from the office of T. G. Jackson) who since 1903 had been Architectural Editor for the Victorian County History. As that body was about the only one with experience of surveying ruins[5] Peers, when confronted by the growing mass of ruins already held by the Office of Works, was no stranger to the situation.[6]

The next ambitious project to produce a cover, not historical, but of ancient monuments and historic buildings, was set up in October 1908 when royal authority was given by Edward VII to:

> appoint commissioners to make an inventory of the Ancient and Historical monuments and Constructions connected with or illustrative of the contemporary culture, civilization and conditions of life of people of England excluding Monmouthshire from the earliest times to 1700 and specify those which seem most worth of preservation...[7]

Monmouthshire was excluded because there were separate commissions for Scotland, and Wales, a division reflected in the later legislation.

The pressure for more legislation was building up being, no doubt, the main motive for Baldwin Brown's book mentioned above. The rather generalised instructions given to the Commissioners led to troubles later since it allowed almost infinite expansion of detail, the rock on which sadly, in the long run, the Commission foundered. As a reference work to assist in the selection of monuments for preservation, a problem on which opinions varied, it was a reasonable step to take. Like all Royal Commissions there was no doubt an element of positive delay assumed before legislation was required, postponing the evil day when decisions on compulsory powers had to be made.

As for its format and content, as a work of reference was it to be short, like a gazetteer? How detailed was the description to be? With the Commissioners being largely academics the pressure to increase the detail became irresistible. This made the object of covering the whole country an ever-receding target and indeed it became clear after the Second World War that it would never be achieved. Broadly speaking, the pre-1914 volumes tended to be too short; between the two world wars a good working size, as for Essex or Herefordshire, was achieved but the huge volumes for Dorset showed that the matter was getting out of hand. The ever-advancing date from 1700 in 1908 brought more and more material into its purview. The abandonment of the parish division (retained by the *VCH*) meant that it was no longer a work of reference but became random, learned volumes on special subjects.

The RCHM had lost its way and had to be closed down or, rather, absorbed into English Heritage. It had indeed found a new role as an archive, its own records combined with those it had acquired, forming a formidable collection of photographs, plans, collections, off-prints and reports now housed at Swindon (in 2006, it is known as the National Monuments Record Centre). It would be wrong to underestimate its impressive lasting achievement. Ruins and earthworks, buildings and field monuments have been furnished with an enormous archive upon which to draw.

The Commission differed from Works preservation in that its inventories covered both inhabited buildings and churches that were still in use, the latter being its staple element. This sort of treatment, so valuable for local antiquaries, provided a model for Sir Nikolaus Pevsner in Penguin's *Buildings of England*, the great survey conducted county by county from the 1950s to the 1970s.[8] This was thorough in its summaries, albeit art-historical, censorious and didactic, and in its original edition it was without ground plans. Ruins were not ignored, although they were not a primary consideration.

* * * * *

Attention must now turn to a politician who played a significant part in the legislation that affected ruins before the First World War and, for a long time, moulded our attitude towards them; Lord Curzon, later Earl Curzon of Kedleston. With an impeccable educational record of Eton, Balliol and All Souls Colleges he was well prepared for the nineteenth-century Empire. He launched his political career as the Conservative MP for Southport, but it is not his politics but his travels that interest us.[9]

He made his first journey around the world in 1887–8 and to Central Asia in 1888. He was in Persia in 1889–90, as a reporter for *The Times,* which resulted in his great two-volume work, still regarded as authoritative, on *Persia and the Persian Question.* In 1894–5 he was in the Pamirs and Afghanistan, normally travelling alone on horseback. Obviously relations with Russia and the 'Great Game' were in his mind, but not the least part of his motivation was an unquenchable thirst for ruins.

A ruin, for him, was the shadow cast by long-vanished greatness, something to be revived and reconstructed in his mind. Nevertheless he had an observant eye and immense appetite for facts.[10]

He was not just a tourist, as he himself says in his first volume on Persia:

I shall not be reproached if I linger awhile amongst these renowned and often commemorated relics of the past…though in dealing with these ancient and historic monuments I shall not recapitulate architectural or topographical details, which can be found better displayed in other more technical works. I shall yet avail myself of the latest scientific knowledge and research.[11]

Chapter XXI in the second volume on Persia, on 'Persepolis, and other Ruins', concludes with a list of six ruins in Persia 'still to be excavated', and it runs to 81 pages. He was almost as much an archaeologist as a politician.

He was particularly interested in the highly-coloured tiled Moslem architecture of Central Asia. 'The Righistan of Samarkand' he declared, 'was even in its ruin the noblest public square in the world.'[12] Readers who have seen it after the Soviet reconstruction will certainly understand his feelings.

Curzon was created Baron Curzon of Kedleston in the Irish peerage in 1898 and was Viceroy of India from 1898 to 1904. This allowed him to exercise his talents on restoration and protection of Indian monuments. In 1901 he said to the Legislative Council:

I have often emphasised what I conceived to be the duty of the Government in this respect and everywhere that I have been throughout India on tour I have made a most careful inspection of the famous or beautiful buildings of the past and have given orders as to their repair or preservation…and as to the appointment of a Director General of Archaeology…[13]

In 1904 he was proceeding with legislation:

The principle of the Bill is the sound, and, as I think, irrefragable proposition that a nation is interested in its antiquities an interest which is based on grounds alike of history, sentiment and expediency and that it reasonable and proper to give statutory sanction to maintenance of this principle by the State…the Government of India has made three mistakes. In the first place they had not recognised that any obligation lay upon them. They had devolved it entirely upon local Government…The third mistake was that conservation or the task of preserving the memorable that we still possess is the task, not of research for those that no longer exist…[14]

The Ancient Monuments Preservation Act, about which Curzon was speaking, '… placed an official seal upon five years of labour which the historian of future time will surely describe as his most enduring work in India.'[15] The greatest of these works was at Agra, but we cannot go into details of his work there. Curzon had no doubt about his own achievement in India:

I am proud to say that the ancient monuments of India are now better preserved and more worthy of a visit than the corresponding structures in any country in the world…[16]

More convincing is the view of an Indian, Pandit Nehru, who is reported to have said to Earl Swanton, Secretary of State for Commonwealth Relations in 1952–5, 'After every other Viceroy has been forgotten Curzon will be remembered because he restored all that was beautiful in India.'[17]

On his return to England in 1905 there is no doubt that Curzon had been profoundly influenced by his experience in India. There was a delay before he could directly influence events. He had chosen an Irish peerage so that he could return to the Commons but he found himself a Conservative in opposition without a seat in either house. In 1908 he was elected Irish representative peer, which gave him a seat in the Lords, and in 1911 he was created Earl of Kedleston.

Tattershall Castle, Lincolnshire, must now be the centre of discussion. It is a moated site, with fragmentary ruins of a thirteenth-century curtain wall and towers and buildings inside.[18] The whole site is dominated by a great brick tower, four storeys high, with octagonal turrets at the corners. The tower is known to have been built by Ralph Lord Cromwell in the 1430s.[19] It would be quite out of place to fully describe this magnificent structure here, but it may be mentioned that the fine machicolation gallery at the top and the traceried windows give it such a very imposing and dignified air that Lord Curzon's attraction to it can be readily understood.[20] Each floor has mantelpieces

Figure 16 *Tattershall Castle keep after restoration by Lord Curzon.*

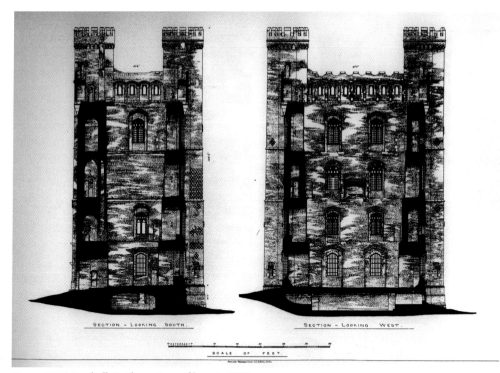

Figure 17 *Tattershall Castle, sections of keep in 1870.*

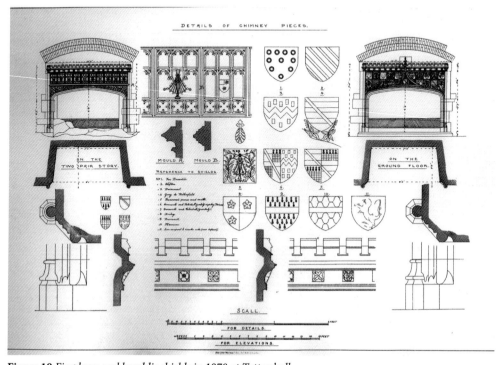

Figure 18 *Fireplaces and heraldic shields in 1870 at Tattershall.*

over the fireplaces, highly decorated, with heraldry on the ground floor. Detailed drawings were made of it in 1870[21] but by the end of the century it was a roofless, floorless ruin, abandoned and sold to a speculator. The dates of events are from *The Times*, which normally refer to the events that happened on the previous day:

5 September 1911	Tattershall mantelpieces reported to have been sold.
11 September 1911	Mantelpieces extracted.
14 September 1911	Appeal for purchasing castle.
16 September 1911	Loan of £5000 offered to National Trust to buy Castle.
20 September 1911	Trust's negotiations fail.
26 September 1911	Mantelpieces removed and fear of rioting.
29 September 1911	Mantelpieces transported to London to secret destination.
30 September 1911	Estate sold.
7 November 1911	Lord Curzon visited and purchased castle.
25 November 1911	Lord Curzon to preserve castle and recover mantelpieces.
22 December 1911	Lord Curzon prepared to negotiate on mantelpieces.
21 May 1912	Lord Curzon has recovered mantelpieces.
5 June 1912	Mantelpieces recovered and will be returned today.
6 June 1912	Mantelpieces returned 'amid public rejoicing'. Lord arrived and stayed with Vicar. A platform erected in front of the tower from which Curzon addressed the crowd for whom he afterwards provided tea.

The feared disorder apparently did not take place at the time of the removal of the mantelpieces. They were brought, by train, back from London and transported by wagon draped with Union Jacks to the castle. The American 'syndicate',[22] who had the mantelpieces hidden in London waiting for export to America, had to be brought under some pressure to give them up. Curzon apparently visited the castle in November 1911 and telegraphed an offer to the owners, which was said to be of £12,000, well beyond what the National Trust could raise.

Curzon's intervention may have been accidental at first, prompted by seeing a photograph, but the political consequences were considerable in view of the impending legislation, which may indeed have been hastened by these events: there were two Bills in the Lords in 1912. The existing legislation was clearly quite incapable of handling a situation of this kind, which demonstrated beyond any further question that the modest compulsory powers Lubbock wanted in his Bill were imperative for any effective legislation. Swift designation, backed by penalties for non-compliance, could not be avoided. Curzon did not ignore the political implications of Tattershall, as we shall see.

The Times reported that, in his address on the platform in front of the tower, Curzon said that he had instructed his architect, William Weir, to recover a full plan of the castle, which after treatment was to be opened to the public. Four years later Curzon purchased the fine moated ruin of Bodiam Castle in Sussex and here also he spent large sums on its treatment as a ruin.[23] He seems to have been quite confident, from the experience he had gained in India, that he knew how to do this. Rather than wishing to 'collect' castles, as his biographers claim with some disbelief, surely it was to some extent a political gesture demonstrating to the Office of Works, who then had no experience of how to lay out a ruin, exactly how to do it. Perhaps they learnt more than is usually admitted.

Almost at the same date as the drama at Tattershall, even more spectacular events took place on the other side of the island at Caernarfon Castle in north Wales, where, following the Coronation of his father, the (first) Investiture of the Prince of Wales (later Duke of Windsor) took place on 12 August 1911. It was a triumph for Lloyd George and brought the Principality into the headlines. As *The Times* leader of the 14 August said:

> Among the brilliant functions of the Coronation period the Investiture of the Prince of Wales is probably the most picturesque and most satisfying to the spectator.

On the previous day, *The Times* devoted six columns to describing the event, with a plan of the seating in the castle and a view of it across the River Seiont.

Academics may well shake their heads about the historicity of the first Investiture, but this is not our concern. It drew general, public attention to Edward I's greatest castle and other ruins of this kind. The ceremony itself, however improbable the costumes, made people think of what might really have or have not happened. A ruin used in this way is not dull. Though not perhaps for *The Times* leader-writers, for much of the general public, in the slightly illusory atmosphere of the late Imperial period, it had real significance.[24]

In more practical terms the preparation of the castle (roofing the Eagle Tower and much else) carried out by a large body of men from, certainly, February (*The Times* 8 and 21 February) had a more permanent effect. They became the work force that afterwards worked in England and Wales on the rapidly growing body of ruins. The recent discovery of a large number of photographs of Stonehenge and other English monuments in the 1920s in the roof space of a private house in Caernarfon, evidently the home of the superintendent of the time, is a reminder of the importance of the castle as a major depot at that time.[25]

It would be tedious in the extreme to follow the Bill that became the Ancient Monuments Consolidation and Amendment Act of 1913, which is memorable for one of Curzon's best speeches and the somewhat unenthusiastic attitude of the First Commissioner of Works, Earl Beauchamp, who introduced it in the Lords. The latter was 'fully aware of the difficulty of the subject' while Curzon was not deterred by these difficulties.[26] The two second readings and the sessions were dominated by Curzon, who revealed his passionate interest in his first speech on the subject. Some long quotations from the Parliamentary Debates of 30 April 1912 give the feeling of the times and the strength of Curzon's own feeling in the matter:

> For my own part I am glad to give support to this Bill, both because this is a matter in which I have taken great interest and because, I think, of those noble lords who sit on this side of the House, I can promise an interest and sympathy equal to my own…This Bill may be regarded as a very subordinate matter in the general scheme of the legislation of the

Government, but to those who take an interest in ancient monuments it is a very important measure, and I came down to the house with the hope of hearing the noble Earl discourse upon it for a period of at least half an hour, and I should have been content to listen to his for an hour but he manages to compress his observations within seven minutes. He treated the Bill as if it were a perfunctory matter…

…The whole attitude of this country and of the civilised world in general has changed towards archaeology in recent years. We regard the national monuments to which this Bill refers as part of the heritage and history of the nation…they are documents just as valuable in reading the record of the past as any manuscript or parchment deed…The case in England is different from what it is in any other country. I know and for this reason. These ancient monuments are dear, not only to ourselves but to our offspring who have gone out from this country to our dominions beyond the seas…the last speaker raised the question of what a national monument is. I take it that the national monuments to which reference is made in this Bill are structural monuments which may be, on the one hand old stone circles and remains, and on the other may be fabrics and by fabrics I mean castles, the castellated structures that recall to us the traditions of feudal times. If you take up any book about monuments of Britain 100 or 150 years ago and compare them with the numbers that now exist you will be horrified at the diminution. Go look at Avebury where you see that magnificent arrangement of stones quite destroyed…This is the fourth Bill relating to this subject which has been placed before Parliament…The Bills to which I refer were very mild and insignificant measures, and I agree with Lord Burghclere that, if this Bill passes into law in its present form, twenty years hence it will be looked upon as a ridiculously mild and inoffensive Bill…

I do not say we ought to be guided by the practice or precedent of foreign countries but I do think it worthwhile to remember that we are far behind in these respects any other civilised society…They take entire control of excavations, and have almost in all cases powers of compulsory expropiation…but let me add that in any thing that fell from my lips on that point I shall not like to be thought to utter one word in disparagement of attitude and conduct of private owners in this country…

I have referred to Avebury and the shocking spoliation and demolition that have taken place there. Let me mention one or two other cases…then there is the case of Tattershall Castle in Lincolnshire. It may interest your Lordships to know that the castle, which is really a beautiful specimen of English brickwork of the fifteenth century I suppose the finest in existence anywhere was sold to an American syndicate for purely speculative purposes. They might have done with it what they willed. The beautiful and historic mantelpieces covered with heraldic bearings of the former owners of Tattershall, were taken out with the object of being sent to America… In these cases the government in the existing condition of affairs is absolutely helpless. All it can do is to sit still and look on while these acts happen; the only power it possesses being the limited and almost futile prerogative given it by the legislation of 1882 and 1900. Public opinion I venture to say is a very insecure guarantee in matters of taste and antiquity and art. For in what way does public opinion act in this matter? It proceeds entirely by fits and starts…

I have made a careful study of the Bill before venturing to speak to your lordships upon it, and I do not think, if I may say so, that the noble Earl in charge of the Bill [Earl Beauchamp] has been altogether wise in the way he has drawn it up…[27]The great part of the Bill is merely consolidation; two thirds or three fourths of it are merely repetition of Acts already on the Statute Book…as I understand there are two new powers taken in the Bill and two only. The first is the right of initiative on the part of the Government to assume control of any monument which may be neglected or in danger of destruction, and the second is the constitution of an Advisory Board to assist the Government in regard to this matter…

The House of Lords was much more of an assembly of landlords than the House of Commons so the use of compulsory purchase to save a monument gave more offence there; Lubbock's Bill had failed in the Commons and was referred to a Committee just before the dissolution in 1880, knowing this would kill it. It was the same issue in 1912–13: they would not accept compulsory purchase so the Government compromise was the Preservation Order. This used guardianship, giving control to the Government but leaving title to the owner. It was a cumbersome, hardly workable solution when it took a compulsory form; this is what Curzon opposed and he spoke from experience. It was the main issue in the debates. It was 60 years, rather than the 20 imagined by Curzon, before the alteration was made. His greater experience when compared to that of the Government is only too apparent in his speech.

The result was that here were to be separate Advisory Boards in Scotland, England and Wales, as the Royal Commission of 1908 had been separated and in due course the organisations became entirely separate under different Ministers. No one in the debate seemed to think that the Bill applied to inhabited buildings and, in the Act, clause 8 says that it will not 'apply to any structure which appears to be occupied as a dwelling house'.[28] Although it covers many other structures, like bridges, that were in use it meant that the Office of Works was principally concerned with ruins and earthworks; the Act was to some extent a charter for ruins, as will be evident in the following chapters.

Notes

1   A description with plan and illustration of the keep at Coucy as it was in the nineteenth century can be found in Viollet-le-Duc's *Dictionnaire*, Vol IV, 264–269.
2   Pugh 1970.
3   The initial volume in each county started with natural history, moving on to earthworks, Roman remains, monastic foundations: in the case of Lincolnshire only the latter was published in volume 2.
4   Thompson 1959.
5   Dated plans, often in colour, are found in the early volumes for some counties, especially for the North Riding of Yorkshire.
6   Dated plans were a feature of Office of Works guidebooks from the First World War onwards.
7   Printed at the front of each volume.
8   The last county to be covered in 1974 was Staffordshire.
9   There are a number of biographies apart from the official three-volume work by the Earl of Ronaldshay 1928: Mosley 1960; Edwardes 1965; Rose 1969; Gilmour 1996. The latter is the most authoritative. The author is less obsessed with the 'imperialist' caricature.
10 Edwardes 1965, 21.
11 Curzon 1892, 10. The political and ethnic detail in the book is formidable.
12 Rose 1969.
13 Curzon 1906. Indian speeches.
14 *ibid.*
15 Ronaldshay 1928, ii, 339.
16 SPAB 1923, p 47.
17 Rose 1969, 339. Curzon's main interests were in the Mogul north of India and he probably regarded the temples in use in south India as not ruinous and so not requiring attention. He had a preference also for Muslim over Hindu architecture, and secular over religious architecture.
18 A. Thompson 1928; M. Thompson 1974; Curzon and Tipping 1929.
19 Simpson 1960. The accounts are not of particulars so they cannot be related exactly to the construction of the tower, which took ten or so years to build. They are primarily concerned with the cost of brick-making.

20 Bearing in mind that we see the tower today after considerable restoration, particularly at the top, as well as repainting of the mantelpieces.

21 F. H. Reed's measured drawings in 1870 give a clear idea of the state of the tower before the events of 1911–12 (figs 17, 18).

22 No information is available about the American syndicate that removed the mantelpieces to London, but it is hoped that future research in the United States might throw some light on this.

23 Curzon 1926. Bodiam Castle, Sussex, is a rectangular moated castle of the late fourteenth century (dated by licence to crenellate), ruinous but with walls standing several feet high. If we except the tower at Tattershall, Bodiam is a much better surviving and exposable structure with its impressive regularity. Both castles were bequeathed by Curzon to the NT.

24 The patriotic ethos of the first Investiture of the Prince of Wales at Caernarvon Castle in 1911 was very different from the second Investiture in 1969, with the early stirrings of Welsh nationalism.

25 The items were purchased from the owner of the house and returned to official archives in London.

26 PD (L) Vol XI 30 April 1912.

27 The title given to the Bill *Ancient Monuments Consolidation and Amendment Bill* certainly bears out Curzon's description.

28 The omission of inhabited buildings, as well as ecclesiastical buildings in use, is of course the reason for the orientation of the Office of Works and its successors towards ruins and earthworks, as well as evidently its preoccupation with the excavation of vanished structures.

Chapter 6

State Preservation of Ruins

Although it was decided to obtain and later publish translations from British embassies in Paris and Vienna of current legislation in France and Hungary to assist in the discussion on proposed legislation in this country, no attention was paid to it in the Bill passed through Parliament in 1913.[1] The most outstanding feature of the difference is that in France preservation of buildings was a matter for the Minister of Fine Arts, while in Hungary it was the responsibility of the Minister of Worship and Education. The difference is so striking that the reasons and merits of the different organisations deserve fuller discussion: it is after all something that puzzles, or used to puzzle, people before the creation of English Heritage in the 1980s.

In France and many parts of the Continent the object was to preserve buildings in use, such as cathedrals, country houses, palaces and so on. In Britain, since 1882, the assumption has been that buildings of aesthetic value in use are maintained by the user, normally the owner. In Britain abandoned buildings, which had become ruinous, were ignored until the public, acting through Parliament, decided to try to preserve them. Ruins rarely have aesthetic value and may be positively ugly, so they hardly required a Fine Arts Department to deal with them. As they required rather special treatment what better arrangement than maintaining them directly with labour provided by the body that already maintained the ancient buildings that were still used by the state for largely ceremonial purposes. It could be said that Fine Arts people usually lack the down-to-earth knowledge that ruins demand. Are the Irish ruins of 1869, the prehistoric ruins of 1882 or the medieval ruins of 1913 proper matters for a Fine Arts Commission? One feels that the Government suggestion in 1880 that ancient monuments be put under the Trustees of the British Museum, which was accepted by Lubbock but knocked down by the Trustees, was not likely to have been successful. The sort of structures being preserved should, to a major degree, determine which organisation is best suited to handle them. English Heritage, for example, deals increasingly with buildings that are still in use so there is every justification for shedding its Works image.

In the nineteenth century, the First Commissioner of Works was an important figure with a seat in the Cabinet. There was no Fine Arts Minister and no real candidate to look after ruins or uninhabited monuments. The Office of Works already employed a large body of craftsmen and labourers so it was merely a question of extending what was already there.

The old Ministry of Works[2] was like a snowball, ever enlarging as it took new responsibilities, particularly of course during the Second World War, and then merging with other ministries into the massive Department of the Environment in the 1970s, when it effectively disappeared as a separate organisation. Part three of Emmerson's book, *The Heritage of the Past*, is divided into three chapters; the first two, 'Royal Parks' and 'Public Buildings', representing traditional functions and the third, entitled 'The State as Guardian of the Past', bringing together historic buildings of the Crown and 'ancient monuments' – the latter, as it were, being an extension of the former. This gives some idea of the extraordinary range of ancient buildings already held by the Crown to which ancient monuments were a relatively minor addition.

The Office of Works was in no sense a professional organisation but a Government ministry, with administrative civil servants over a large professional and industrial staff below. In Ancient Monuments, the architects had a senior architect in charge and they controlled the scattered industrial staff with its regional organisation headed by a superintendent, a craftsman by origin acting as a sort of sergeant major. The historical expertise was supplied by a Chief Inspector and his staff of Inspectors. Needless to say a very different organisation has come about since an independent Commission, English Heritage, was created outside Government.

There is no more revealing indication of the extent to which Works saw itself as a continuation of the Crown's medieval and later organisation than the six (seven with the box of plans) great volumes of *The History of the King's Works* (HMSO), commissioned in 1951, the first two volumes, dealing with the medieval period, appearing in 1963.[3] The general editor and partial author was Sir Howard Colvin and, except for the Chief Inspector, Arnold Taylor, most of the contributors were from outside, with the Ministry providing support services. The Public Record Office was scoured to produce this very splendid and monumental achievement. As the Minister of Works wrote at the beginning of the first volume:

> As heir to the responsibilities of the officer of Royal Works throughout the centuries I am privileged to present these first two volumes of a history of royal building and its organisation in this country.[4]

This fitting memorial to Works was completed at about the same time as Works itself disappeared into the Department of the Environment. There is of course a large measure of continuity with ancient monuments even into English Heritage, which tries hard to appear different.

It is difficult to envisage the situation that confronted Charles Peers in 1910. He had quite a lot of experience of ruins as the architectural editor for a then very active Victoria County History. In the first two Inspector's Reports, 1911 and 1912, he was dealing with urgent repairs on the rapidly growing number of ruins for which he was responsible.[5] An article by William J. Davies in the journal of the Royal Institute of British Architects, which had earned him a silver medal, sets out the position:

> …nothing in the nature of restoration in its modern and, of recent years, odious sense was attempted and that everything of the past is worthy of preservation at all costs has been of very gradual and of comparatively late growth.[6]

The argument against restoration is simple; faithful restoration is impossible. Historical science leads its support to the desire to retain everything of the past. The architect has several courses open to him – he can follow the old restorers, take advice of anti-restorers or, the most logical course, do nothing:

If the monument is not fulfilling its original purpose, it is evident that the only reason for preserving it is as an illustration of artistic and historic development. As such the less done to it the better; only those things necessitated by maintaining it in no worse state than it has already reached…[7]

Excavation for research is justified. 'A museum can never take the place of a monument in educational value.'[8]

Davies has given us the best justification for how and why ruins should be preserved, which holds good today as it did in 1913. Peers would have seen the article in his own professional journal and we may suspect it influenced his actions. Davies regarded the preservation function as an educational one and so logically it should not be in the hands of the Office of Works but in a Ministry of Public Education. He ended his article with the well-known quotation from Montalembert : *Les longs souvenirs font les grands peuples.*

That Peers had been influenced by Davies is suggested by his paper in the same journal in 1931, 21 years after he first took office.[9] In that he states that we have to accept old and new. The beauty of a building does not reside in its age but its history, its varied fortune. If a building is in use it is unreasonable to treat it as a museum but where its active life is ended work is conducted in a different spirit. In a ruin, what is left is a fraction of what was there and so is especially precious. Work on it is not creative but re-creative. Nothing should be either added or taken away without due cause.

Peers went on to describe work at four of the major undertakings of the Office of Works in the 1920s: Byland Abbey, Yorkshire; Goodrich Castle, Herefordshire; Furness Abbey, Lancashire; and Rievaulx Abbey, Yorkshire. Each of these four ruins had been the scene of very large retrieval operations at the time – characteristically, three of them

Figure 19 *Rievaulx Abbey in the 1920s before retrieval.*

Figure 20 *Rievaulx Abbey after retrieval.*

were monastic sites. The finer quality of the architecture, the more easily understood plan and the greater fame of the monument gave them a higher priority.

> What we do in the buildings is largely routine work, and the technical preservation is a secondary thing compared with the preservation of the spirit of the buildings themselves.[10]

Some of what Peers had to say we would expect: 'Repair must neither deface nor obscure old work'. There is, however, one fundamental observation overlooked by later practitioners that clearly will have to be faced in the future: 'The life of a building can be prolonged but not indefinitely'.[11]

An unroofed ruin with walls exposed and freed from fallen debris and vegetation is at the mercy of the very hostile British weather; treatment has to be repeated after so many years but the fabric cannot last forever. This might be an argument for making use of the ruin in whatever way possible during its lifetime; it might even be an argument for 'restoration'.

This may be a matter for discussion or even action by English Heritage but here it is a distraction from the main story. After the First World War, the Office of Works had a reasonably coherent and defensible policy in relation to the ruins in its care, a policy logically and politically justifiable because it was the cheapest solution that would least offend anybody. The general outlook has lasted to the present day and has certainly influenced many countries abroad, although often as an ideal that was not

Figure 21 *Byland Abbey before retrieval in the 1920s.*

Figure 22 *Byland after retrieval.*

always realisable. The passive attitude required was not always reconcilable for those who saw the monuments in terms of patriotism.

There is another matter belonging to the early decades of the last century that deserves our attention. To what extent were the attitudes of the Office of Works moulded by the views of Morris, 'Anti-Scrape' and SPAB? Obviously the whole ethos of architecture at that period had been influenced by these. Curzon, for example, was an active member of SPAB. Nevertheless, the more puritanical aspects of SPAB, like the use of broken tile coursing to replace removed, decayed masonry (broadly regarded as a joke) was not copied, and restoration for structural or protective reasons was used much more freely than by the SPAB. A more flexible practice was adopted. Arts and Crafts influence is clear in certain aspects of carpentry (wooden pegs) or in mortar mixes.

Between 1935 and 1975 there was a transformation in archaeology, particularly in prehistory but affecting all periods and in due course creating new ones, such as industrial archaeology. This has been associated with all sorts of new techniques other than excavation, such as air photography, that have allowed us to appreciate much better what is underground. Ruins and earthworks have become merely the visible part of the iceberg. Those periods which lack written records have benefited most, not only in numbers employed in their study but in the whole attitude towards the past.

It is very instructive to compare the concerns that Peers expressed, when he first took office, in the first (and only) three Inspector's Reports of 1910–13, with the Reports of the Advisory Boards, which, though created in 1913, apparently only published reports from 1954, following the 1953 Act. The first thing that strikes one is the predominance, particularly among nominated members, of archaeologists, especially prehistorians. It was like a prehistorians's conference within a body whose main function was maintaining medieval ruins. In 1910–13 Peers had merely made a distinction between the prehistoric monuments of 1882 and the growing number of these monuments with the individual treatment of which he was almost exclusively concerned about, at that time, in England, Scotland and Wales.

Prehistorians take a lofty attitude towards periods that possess written sources and so in 1954 medieval monuments were virtually ignored and there was a preoccupation with 'scheduling', designating in the Choay sense, of earthworks, especially burial mounds. No doubt it was useful to bring a vast number of such monuments within the protective umbrella of the Act, although no real solution has been found to protect such remains from ploughing. It is as frustrating as protecting masonry remains from the weather.

If prehistoric remains were the main concern in the 1950s and 1960s, a dramatic change followed the advancement, more or less to the present day, of what might be regarded as national monuments.[12] Military defences from the Second World War and industrial monuments greatly increased the field of what ought to be protected. It also altered views on not only what, but how monuments should be preserved. Windmills, or machinery generally, are best appreciated if actually working. This requires restoration. If all the remains of material culture from all periods are documents of contemporary life then almost everything is worthy of preservation; it is an alarming thought!

The growth in archaeology, and the belief that excavation could produce valid historical information, has given rise to 'rescue' archaeology, the survey and excavation of areas threatened by development before it takes place. From relatively small beginnings during the war on the sites of proposed aerodromes, the volume of rescue archaeology has grown exponentially, at first undertaken by the Ministry itself but now in the hands of archaeological contractors, the former regional trusts, which have become self-financing bodies with money paid by the developers.

The whole ethos of the organisation has been transformed by the archaeological shift in the spectrum. The statutory Inspector of 1882, Pitt-Rivers, was an archaeologist and with the exception of the crucial figure of Peers, an architect, his successors have been archaeologists. Inspectors lost their statutory status in 1979 and the post of Chief Inspector was suppressed shortly afterwards. A new non-statutory figure of Chief Archaeologist has emerged. Needless to say the attitude towards ruins has altered considerably, with the need for investigation archaeologically at all stages of treatment regarded as essential, as well as on monuments already laid out, as for example by Dr Glyn Coppack revealing the very early stages of the foundation of the great Cistercian Abbey at Fountains, Yorkshire.[13] A ruin indeed comes into its own in a project like this – the whole extent of the site is accessible in a way that is often not possible in an occupied building, where the interference would be intolerable for the occupants. This is indeed one of several advantages offered to researchers by these sites.

As a counterbalance to the growth of archaeology, which has so affected ruins, almost at the same time measures have been taken to extend protection to inhabited buildings, so rigorously excluded from the purview of the Office of Works in 1913. The widespread destruction of dwellings by bombing during the Second World War not surprisingly led to solicitude for those that survive. Buildings in use allow the art historian to exercise his talents and it is not too much to say that, led by Sir Nikolaus Pevsner, this new attitude to buildings in use has quite altered the way we looked at them before the war.

Planning legislation, not the Ancient Monuments Acts, has been the instrument for preserving inhabited buildings. It is not necessary to become entangled in its complexity especially since its implementation is largely in the hands of Local Authorities at county and district level.[14] The designation of a building as a 'historic building', the equivalent of the national monument of Mme Choay, is distinguished from 'scheduling' by the division into three grades. The chances of survival, or of obtaining money for repair, is very much dependent on the grading. The other feature of interest is the 'Conservation Area', which covers a group of buildings. This may offer protection to a ruin in the area or, more importantly, help it retain sympathetic surroundings.

The history of conservation in Britain since the war has been partly one of ancient monuments and historic buildings being drawn together, with a reliance upon planning legislation, even if the requirements of occupied and unoccupied structures are very different. The language is either archaeological or art historical, with very different sorts of vocabulary – to use a favourite word of the art historians. There is a very practical basis for the distinction between Historic Building 'listing' and 'scheduling', even if French logic suggests they are the same thing.[15]

Notes

1   Report 1914, Cmd 7151. The translations received from ambassadors in Paris and Vienna were available in 1912 before publication.
2   The title of 'Office' was raised to 'Ministry' during the First World War and has been described by Emmerson 1965. Works did not entirely disappear until the 1970s when a new body, the Public Service Agency, was created.

3 Sir Howard Colvin (ed.) 1963.

4 *ibid,* at beginning of volume 1.

5 *Reports of Inspector of Ancient Monuments* 1911, 1912, 1913. Cmd. 5960, 6510, 7258.

6 Davies 1913. Published in the year of the Act, this valuable article is entirely free of any sycophantic attitude and no doubt represented the feelings of many architects at the time. Its logic is convincing.

7 *ibid,* 594.

8 *ibid,* 597.

9 Peers 1931.

10 *ibid,* 325.

11 *ibid,* 320.

12 If ruins means disused structures in an advanced state of dereliction and decay for which there is no possibility of reuse then these relatively modern structures have to be regarded as monuments: if they arose from an important event or technical advance then they can also be treated as national monuments, albeit not very ancient.

13 Coppack and Gilyard-Beer 1986.

14 Although out of date, Kennet 1972 shows the difficulties.

15 Choay 2000.

Chapter 7

Intelligibility[1]

After the woodwork has gone, the roofs and floors, the shapes in which the masonry survives is completely fortuitous. Apart from the incessant assault by wind, rain, frost and the growth of vegetation, ivy shrubs and even trees, there may be human intervention, particularly at the lower levels, to extract stone for reuse, which was valuable in stoneless areas. The first problem with a ruin then, as opposed to what confronts the viewer of an intact building, is to determine what the remains belong to, what the building was whose decay gave rise to these fantastic forms. The shapes are not only puzzling but often, from risk of collapse, dangerous as well.

In approaching an intact building one is normally faced with a formal frontage of some kind, usually designed deliberately to indicate what is behind. We tend to make an immediate judgement of the building from its elevation, and its lack in a ruin makes it so difficult to reconcile ourselves to it. It may be that the removal of ivy reveals a significant feature like a doorway or traceried window that allows us to restore, to some extent, in our mind's eye some semblance of the missing elevation. Nevertheless it is the absence of a complete elevation of the original building that we crave that frustrates us.

The estate agent normally supplies the ground plan of a house to the prospective purchaser with dimensions of rooms and so on. For most of us (architects excluded) it is only in a house purchase that the crucial nature of the ground plan is apparent. One feature that a ruin and a new building share in common is a ground plan; even if the foundations have been robbed out it should be possible to establish the full plan of a ruin. It has the advantage of accessibility, so not only the final plan but alterations along the way can be recovered – it may have been enlarged, reduced or completely rebuilt or a wooden building may have been replaced by a stone one and so on. Few buildings have remained entirely unaltered. Building archaeology is then, to a great extent, chasing ground plans, hoping, of course, that some datable or otherwise significant material will turn up at the same time. For these purposes a ruin is usually easier to study than an occupied building.

The intelligibility of the remains in a ruin depends almost entirely upon a ground plan so that the visible fragments can be related to it. A shapeless lump of masonry, the springing for a vault, a doorway, a pier base and so on become intelligible in relation to the building that has largely vanished. The objective then is to achieve a full ground plan, preferably with approximate dating for different parts; it is an archaeological procedure. This is to jump the gun since there are clearly earlier steps to be taken to maximise intelligibility.

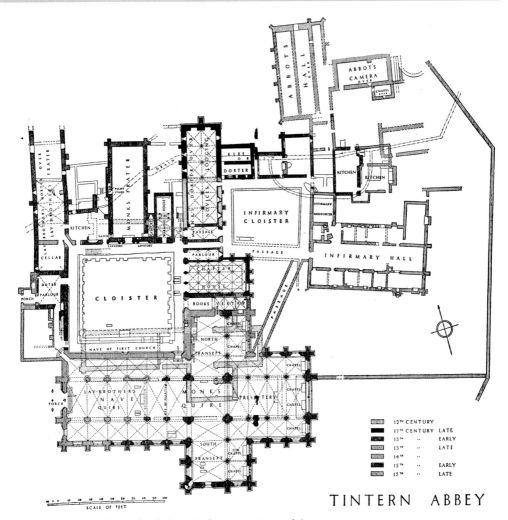

Figure 23 *Tintern Abbey; dated plan. (Cadw, Crown Copyright)*

I have discussed the earlier stages of treatment of ruins twenty years ago[2] but will have to briefly repeat some of what I said there. The word 'retrieval' was used to mean freeing the remains from what has accrued on them since the original building was abandoned. This means removing the overburden largely created by the collapsed structure but also vegetable and soil accumulation from agriculture, dumping, and later structures such as cowsheds. The site may even have been landscaped. Obviously there will be types of monument where retrieval is not necessary; those erected as monuments themselves, such as prehistoric burial mounds, where the mound commemorates or honours the deceased buried in it, do not need retrieval. This applies to standing stones or crosses but not to megalithic monuments.

Roman monuments, such as amphitheatres, will obviously require major retrieval but it is really with medieval monuments that retrieval comes into its own. The depth of debris will obviously vary, from around 0.5 to 5 metres. The labour involved on a large monument can be considerable, the disposal of such large quantities of waste being an additional problem.

Figure 24 Castle Acre Priory; air photograph. Photo: Aerial Archaeology

The considerable effort that is involved is well repaid by the transformation of the site that has taken place. Walls that had disappeared reappear and all existing walls are increased correspondingly in height. The level of the ground should be roughly what it was when the site was abandoned. Something like an intelligible plan should by then have emerged. Even in a monument where the walls stand to full height, like Conway or Caernarvon Castles, all sorts of evidence for vanished internal buildings will come to light.

The matter has been discussed at length in my earlier book[3] and here the illustrations of the naves of Rievaulx and Byland Abbey churches may be repeated (Figures 19–22), showing them as they were before and as they were after the great retrieval operations of the 1920s. The bases of the piers have emerged to make intelligible the form of the original arcades while at Byland the cloister layout has been revealed. It must have been a very satisfying experience during the work but here attention may be confined to a major piece of retrieval that had hardly started when my earlier book was published.

The meticulous excavation and exposure of the deeply buried structures of Dolforwyn Castle, near Newtown, Powys, just beyond Offa's Dyke in Wales[4] have, after 20 years, just reached a successful completion with formal opening to the public. Dr Lawrence Butler, the excavator, has kindly allowed me to use the drawings and photographs in the figures (Figures 26–28). The castle is of interest in that it is a native Welsh one, different from the contemporary English examples. Built by Llywelyn ap Gruffydd in 1273, it was captured by the English in 1277, who occupied it for a period. It is quite small and narrow, roughly 75m long by 39m wide. Its plan was quite uncertain before retrieval. Longitudinal and transverse sections show the depth of overburden largely produced by the disintegration of the poor, laminated shale walls of which it is constructed. The

Figure 25 *Castle Acre Priory; view across cloister.*

rectangular keep at the southern end and the round tower at the northern end had been entirely concealed by the debris and their discovery was unsuspected. A plan (Figure 27) showing all the internal buildings has therefore emerged from the work where only amorphous mounds existed before. A reconstruction drawing (Figure 28) made when work was still unfinished shows how the imagination might recreate it. This is a very model of retrieval as it should be carried out today and can give an idea of the extraordinarily meaningful and fruitful results that even the most unpromising buried site can yield. It may be added that there was valuable dating evidence from coins and other small finds which tallied with the written evidence.

The remains exposed in the retrieval have to be preserved, which is after all the legal reason for doing the work at the monument. The main object is to stabilise and consolidate the ruin. The top of the masonry has to be waterproofed with lime mortar, which is reused in the repointing of any walls that may need underpinning. Ferroconcrete beams may have to be inserted, concealed in the walls. This, more prosaic, work need not be discussed here since the motive is not primarily intelligibility.

More directly concerned with heightening intelligibility is the attempt to put the monument's immediate surroundings into a condition resembling as closely as possible that which existed when the building was in active use. Unless there are cobbles, or evidence for them, smooth mown grass is the usual method used to ensure that plinths and bases of walls, that have just been exposed, and of course thresholds of doors, are not hidden. Some lines of walls may just be marked out and long grass or shrubs would easily conceal them.

On approaching a country house today one passes through extensive parks and gardens and no doubt medieval castles had similar amenities long since vanished. The

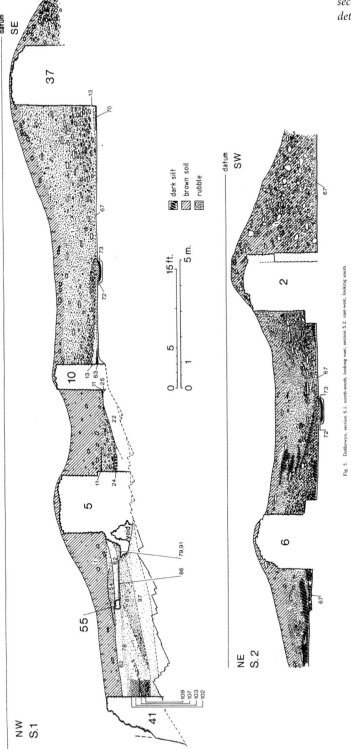

Figure 26 *Dolforwyn Castle; sections through overburden of detritus.*

datum

SE

37

13

70

67

73

72

dark silt

brown soil

rubble

15 ft.

5 m.

5

0

1

0

10

13

11 63

25

22

11

24

5

void

79,91

86

81

61

6

97

55

78

109

107

103

102

41

NW

S.1

datum

SW

67

2

67

73

72

6

67

NE

S.2

Fig. 5. Dolforwyn, section S.1. north-south, looking east; section S.2. east-west, looking south.

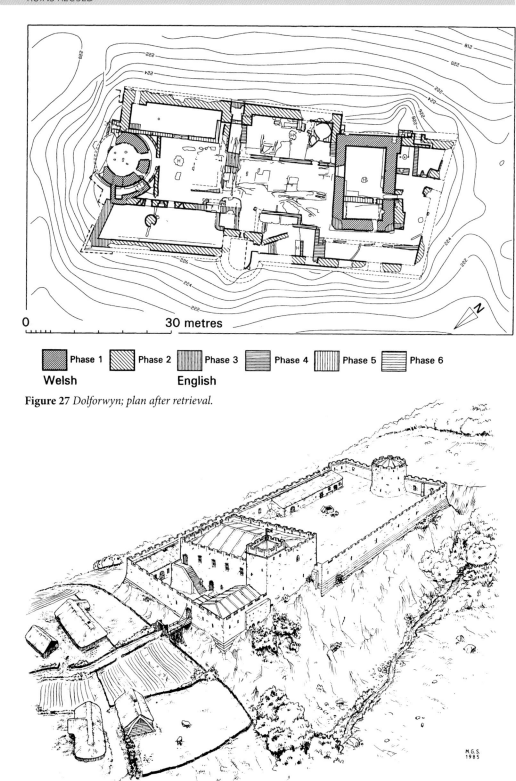

Phase 1 Phase 2 Phase 3 Phase 4 Phase 5 Phase 6

Welsh   English

Figure 27 *Dolforwyn; plan after retrieval.*

Figure 28 *Dolforwyn; Notional reconstruction after retrieval.*

best one can do is to enter by the original access, by the gatehouse if it survives. The psychological affect of approaching an abbey through the gatehouse/bell-tower facing the west end of the church, as at Peterborough, is considerable. The transfer of the entry at Kenilworth Castle, mainly to create a new car park, so that the visitor becomes aware of the massive water defences, even if not yet restored, profoundly affects one's response to the great castle.

Nearly all defensive structures from prehistoric times onwards relied on a ditch excavated around the perimeter as its first line of defence. To remove the later filling and expose this ditch in its original breadth and depth at once enhances the castle or town wall or earthen bank behind it. In towns where the line of the ditch has been used as an inner ring road, the wall itself, particularly if badly preserved, loses some of its force: it gives an illusion that the wall is much higher than it actually is. If the ditch is water-filled, forming a moat, then the results are even more dramatic. Lord Curzon was well aware of this, as the splendid moats of Bodiam and Tattershall remind us.[5] The sparkle and movement of the water seems to bring the ruin to life. There are many examples that come to mind: Beaumaris in Anglesey, Kirby Muxloe in Leicestershire, Leeds Castle in Kent or Caerphilly Castle in Glamorgan (Figures 32–34)

Internal access within the monument requires the provision of stairs, steps and bridges, which have disappeared from the original but have to be replaced for circulation. Something in sympathy without the absurdity of trying to copy the original is what is needed. They tend to form a very distinctive feature of monuments in care.

If the devices just described are intended to enhance the illusion and, at the same time, the intelligibility of the ruin then we must turn to the other side, where conscience does not allow us to heighten the illusion but quite the reverse. When it is intended to indicate

Figure 29 *Avebury; representation of missing standing stones of circle.*

Figure 30 *Woodhenge; representation of vanished timber uprights.*

Figure 31 *Jarrow monastery; representation of walls at different periods.*

that something is missing, but we do not wish to deceive the onlooker by making a false imitation in the gap, then a modern substitute can be used, not unsympathetic to the original but patently not the original. The onlooker is meant to understand from this that the original has been lost.

The most extreme example of this is where the original structure was of wood, which has of course completely disappeared. An excavation has found a pattern of postholes in the subsoil, evidently sockets for uprights, but the height, form or function of these uprights is quite unknown. Many conjectural reconstructions are possible but we have no real idea of the form of the original structure. Low concrete bollards are a possible device, leaving the imagination to try out different solutions; a good example is Woodhenge in Wiltshire, at the end of the Avebury Avenue,[6] where the postholes have been marked out in this fashion (Figure 30).

It is not just wood that has disappeared. At the famous site of Avebury many of the stones forming the circles and avenues have vanished, but of course the sockets they stood in can be located and markers created to indicate where they stood. Nothing has been falsified and the onlooker can be confident he is not being deceived. There are many other occasions when representation is required; if, for example, the removal of a door or window has left a big hole but the shape of the original is not known, the space can be filled with recessed brickwork plastered over.

By far the most common use of 'representation' is in marking out features that have disappeared or distinguishing walls of different periods. Most medieval buildings underwent either enlargement or reduction in size, or both. Earlier wooden buildings can be marked out. Many different materials may be used. There may be a need to show existing earlier features at a lower level by marking the finished ground surface of the monument.

It may be useful to refer to Continental practice, as described by Ulbert and Weber, prompted by a conference arising from the creation of an 'Archaeological Park or Garden' at Kempton (Bavaria). Some very interesting ideas were put forward about work carried out there.[7] It was largely confined to Roman sites, mainly in German-speaking areas and, with the exception of Trier, it dealt with the display of low remains on open sites. Each area is usually defined by a ditch and wall and there is a complete

Figure 32 *Bodiam Castle; water to enhance realism (Lord Curzon).*

77

Figure 33 *Nunney Castle; use of water to set off masonry.*

Figure 34 *Beaumaris Castle as it was.*

Figure 35 *Beaumaris Castle after retrieval and flooding of moat* .

restoration of gates or walls, and occasionally buildings inside. 'Representation' is not used and low walls are reconstructed to a uniform level regardless of gaps in survival. Tidiness and regularity seem to be overriding considerations. The contrast with English treatment of Hadrian's Wall where the high standing core is meant to be exactly as found is remarkable. In England, Ruskin still rules, even if the facing stones had to be numbered and taken down before replacement.

Restoration or complete reconstruction is freely used and while Saalburg, restored in 1900, is described as *falsch,* surely this could be applied to many restorations, including that in the archaeological parks like the proposals at Kempton. The self-confidence is worthy of Viollet-le-Duc.[8] The idea of the archaeological garden or park is an interesting one but surely a highly artificial one only applicable to open Roman sites. Is the cost justified even if the children like it? The pity is that the real Roman buildings, splendid ones at Trier, are in an existing modern town in a contemporary environment.

Some buildings erected to protect vulnerable remains like that at Sargans are of great interest and would deserve much more detailed discussion than can be given here. One area where we could learn most from our Continental colleagues is the organisation of preservation bodies – it is very different from that in this country and arranged on a more regional basis.

The ultimate measure in intelligibility of a ruin is to rebuild it. The snag is that no rebuilding can be certainly, or even probably, the same as what was there originally: put simply we do not know either the form of the original in most cases and the alterations it underwent in any case. Once one starts rebuilding one moves from one guess to the next, each leading to further uncertainty. Even with Roman military buildings, where there is a high degree of conformity, there is uncertainty; the reconstruction of the buildings just described in Germany are essentially copies from what is known elsewhere, although

Figure 36 *Cardiff Castle; restoration of Roman gate by Marquess of Bute. Only the light bottom courses are original.*

they often no doubt bore very close resemblances to what they purport to be. Restoration is still as much of a 'lie' in 2006 as it was for Ruskin in 1850.

The brilliant restorations for the Marquess of Bute by William Burges have been mentioned above (pp.31–2). The castle of Castell Coch (Figure 11) is taken for a medieval castle by most visitors or television cameramen, who do not appreciate that virtually the whole structure is a Victorian creation. It is a tour de force but really a monument to William Burges, not the medieval builders who erected the castle on whose foundations it stands. The objective of legislation since 1882 has been to preserve existing monuments, not create new ones!

We can see at once why the State did not restore monuments: it is not merely the impossibility of accuracy but also the cost and reluctance to create brand new monuments which will require maintenance, presumably quite indefinitely. Restoration on a small scale may be necessary for structural reasons, to hold the building up or to conceal modern supports. More extensive restoration may be necessary to reroof buildings in order to protect wall paintings or other vulnerable items. In the case of industrial monuments, particularly with machinery, complete restoration may be necessary. These are the principles that currently guide work but of course there is a new school of thought today that wants more extensive restoration.

It is very interesting to contrast the views in *c.*1865 of Viollet-le-Duc (Appendix 1) with advice on restoration formulated in the charter of 1964 of the International Congress of Architects and Monument Technicians at Venice (Appendix 6). Viollet-le-Duc, in the full excitement of the discovery of Gothic architecture after the Revolution, regarded restoration as a new discovery and clearly saw it as the answer in all cases. Some of his surviving restorations, like Pierrefonds, have been severely criticised, although the present author certainly found his work at Carcassone very interesting. Over-confidence was clearly Viollet-le-Duc's main problem.

The Charter of 1964 shows how completely attitudes had changed in the hundred years since Viollet-le-Duc. It refers more to Classical monuments than medieval ones although no distinction is presumably intended. Restoration is adopted only as an 'exceptional measure' although not forbidden altogether. The changes since Viollet-le-Duc could hardly be greater and we may presume that the constant attack on restoration by Ruskin and Morris had played some part in this change. In Germany, as we have seen, large-scale restoration on Roman sites, even where nothing visible exists, is practised. It has been suggested that the destructive climate of northern Europe requires different attitudes to those in the Mediterranean area, an argument that is not wholly convincing.

The motive for restoration today is not so much intelligibility as education or tourism. For children particularly, whether the monument is genuine is immaterial provided that it is roughly realistic; we have mentioned the popularity of Castell Coch or Saalburg (p.31) Some fairly fundamental issues are raised about the purpose of preservation: are the monuments 'documents' or simply there to be turned into attractions? How in fact are ruins to be used?

As we have seen since the time of Peers it has been recognised that ruins, even those preserved by English Heritage, do not have an indefinite life; a point must come when either you restore or you lose the monument. This, it is seems to the author, is the only justification for wholesale restoration; the only problem is to decide at what point the level of decay has been reached where the monument will be lost without complete restoration.

Enough has been said to show that after the ruin has been consolidated the main objective is to maximise the understanding or intelligibility of the remains to the onlooker. For an ordinary visitor, unfamiliar with the layout of a monastery, the fragments will be bewildering. He or she cannot understand them without effort. The objective of the 'monument technician', to use the expression in the Charter, is to make it as easy as possible, without damaging the remains or adding more modern material to them than is absolutely necessary, to preserve them on the one hand or render them intelligible to the onlooker on the other. Some visitors may not wish to make the effort and will not be prepared to do so. This is to be expected and is indeed quite natural so there is no need to inflict alterations or even damage on the monument in the vain hope of enticing them to change their minds.

Notes

1   Much of this chapter is covered in Thompson 1981.
2   *ibid,* chapter 4.
3   *ibid*
4   Butler 1989 and 1995.
5   Curzon 1926 and Curzon and Tipping 1929.
6   Thompson 1981, 73.

7   Ulbert and Weber 1985. Mr B. Nurse, Librarian of the Society of Antiquaries, London, kindly drew my attention to this book, which is not readily available in this country.

8   In fairness to the editors of the book, which covers many projects, they themselves discuss the matter in the last chapter and have many misgivings about the creation of entirely artificial archaeological 'parks' or 'gardens' as to whether they are forms of Disneyland. The recreation of buildings like this is only feasible on open Roman military sites where a) the uniformity of Roman buildings allows plausible reproductions and b) there are no later medieval remains to break the illusion. The impressive reproduction of Roman gates and walls at Cardiff Castle by the Marquess of Bute (Fig. 36) could not be turned into an archaeological garden because the remains are inextricably mixed up with the medieval castle as restored by Burges.

Chapter 8

Conclusion

In an extremely interesting book published in 2002,[1] Richard Bradley described the survival of the past or rather remembrance of the past in prehistoric societies. The evidence comes from the juxtaposition of later remains with earlier ones and he makes a good case. There may well be further ethnographic evidence for this. One must ask, is there anything similar in modern society comparable to the attitude just described in prehistoric societies?

In prehistoric times people were living in a largely uninhabited or very lightly inhabited countryside where the forces of nature were still largely dominant. Earlier works of man were few and rapidly engulfed by vegetation, the more conspicuous remains surviving as landmarks and no doubt worked into the religion as the haunt of benign ancestors, gods or devils. Memory was inextricably tied up with religion. One can surely agree with Bradley that there was a conscious attachment to – I hesitate to say memory of – the past, which influenced their actions in the present.

The cut-off period is presumably the Roman Empire, when towns and roads were artificially created. The points of reference were completely altered as well as much of the material culture, even among the native peoples. Unaffected areas, like Ireland, no doubt continued as before, where long memories still survive. The *Völkerwanderung* completed the alienation by the introduction of large numbers of strangers into the countryside. An early Anglo-Saxon poem suggests a complete divorce from what went before:

> Splendid is the masonry-the fates destroyed it
> the stone buildings crashed the work of giants mouldered away
> the roofs have fallen, the towers are in ruins…[2]

The poet may be referring to Bath.

When land became private property and an article of exchange the peasantry living on great estates were alienated from the countryside and its visible remains. Urbanised industrial society carried this even further. As a result, nearly all the preservation that we deal with in this book was not spontaneous from below but imposed from above, *de haut en bas.*

The ecclesiastical ruins transferred to the Irish Board of Works by the Irish Church Act of 1869 (p.34) were, no doubt, the exception. While it would be wrong to suggest that there was a popular movement to have them taken into care, we may suspect that the government included this provision in the Act because it feared that there might be. The terms used to describe them – 'ruin' or 'national monument' – gave ruins an official status, as it were, accidentally.

Otherwise we are dealing with an intellectual concept imposed by law, by Parliament. In the case of Lubbock, a glance at the Schedule (Appendix 3) of the 1882 Act can leave no reasonable doubt that it was the monuments, illustrating the antiquity of man, that were uppermost in his mind. The concepts of Ruskin, albeit never materialising in legislation, were highly intellectual: the sacred nature of the original stonework making 'restoration' a form of blasphemy, not against religion but in terms of aesthetics. The driving force behind the 1913 Act was probably the extent to which the country had fallen behind the Continent and, like prohibiting bear-baiting, it was something that all civilised countries ought to do. This is not to overlook Curzon hammering at the government (he was in opposition), demonstrating his love affair with a ruin at Tattershall. His views were clear for he had just had his own legislation in India; it was the evident duty of Empire to protect the built culture of its subjects. In many respects Curzon is the hero of our book, the rare politician who loved ruins – and restoration at Agra and Tattershall.

In subsequent legislation, fortuitous circumstance was the main mover and the intellectual element in the earlier course of events was not present; the idea of preservation by law was accepted, albeit often reluctantly. It was still imposed from above although the advance and popularity of archaeology have certainly led to a greater understanding and support for legislation.

The growth of tourism has altered the whole picture. It is not merely the individual monuments, nor one may add the smaller monuments, which often tend to be ignored, but monuments collectively as a benefit to the tourist trade generally, for their attraction to foreign tourists who bring foreign currency with them. Indeed, to hear politicians speaking of monuments one might think that their purpose was simply to generate tourism; gone are the lofty ideals of preservation as a civic duty and responsibility in the 'consumer society' of today.

The more one deals with ruins the more one realises how difficult it is to state any general rules that cover them. The first point to establish, as Viollet-le-Duc (Appendix 1) tells us, is to find out how the building or structure is going to be used. If a bridge or town hall, this is presumably not in doubt. These are not the subject of this book since ruins can be defined for our purposes not merely as roofless or fragmentary structures but buildings in a state of decay for which there is no foreseeable function. This was a distinction at once apparent to Peers.[3] If a building is to be used then its function has to be an overriding consideration in any work carried out, but in a structure that has no further use then the object is to 'freeze' what is genuine – that is, consolidate it. 'Restored' work on a ruin is a deception carried out on the onlooker, in the Ruskin sense. Indeed, in many ways the Ruskin/Morris interpretation is more valid on a ruin than on a building in use, where considerable restoration may be essential for the building to function.

The ruin, of course, has its purpose, to remind us of those who erected it originally, a monument in fact. If it has this use, might one not argue that on some occasions it cannot perform this function without some degree of restoration? The point can be illustrated by the Great Wall of China. The tourist is taken to a section near Beijing that is an entirely modern reconstruction. It is a curious work, not following contours but crests, and so has very steep slopes; on television, distinguished visitors are seen trudging up and down these slopes unaware of the fact that they are on a largely modern construction.[4] If one goes to the end of the reconstruction or 'restoration', done on a relatively small length, the wall is hardly recognisable. Still unexposed, it is collapsed, overgrown and much lower than the part open to the public. The reconstruction with its broad walkway and towers follows no doubt the form of the last reconstruction while in use in the fifteenth century. Is there no other way of appreciating the wall's grandeur except by massive reconstruction of a short length? This is no doubt a matter for discussion but I am inclined to think there is not. It might be that an adjoining length treated, but not restored, would help the visitor to appreciate its real condition and the extent to which he is being 'deceived' in the Ruskinian sense.

The contrast with Hadrian's Wall is complete, which is 'treated as found' – very laboriously resetting the numbered face stones with the surviving core sticking up in the middle. You cannot walk on this and it is normally low with no indication that it stood to 5–6 metres high originally, a point that bewilders visitors. What one sees is the genuine survival and not a to some extent hypothetical reconstruction resembling that seen on the Great Wall in China. The trouble is that the visitor wants to see something like his preconception – a big wall – and the fact that it does not survive in this form is not very satisfying.

∗   ∗   ∗   ∗   ∗

Looking back over 500 years, there has always been an interest in ruins among educated people at least: Leland, Camden, Dugdale. For them it was the association with a person or institution that mattered, a monastery or king and so on. Even the Buck brothers

Figure 37 *Hadrian's Wall, scarcely visible on the left.*

Figure 38 *Exposed treated base of Hadrian's Wall at Heddon-on-the-Wall.*

in the eighteenth century drew a ruin or intact building indifferently since it was the association that mattered.

Only with Colt Hoare, through picturesque spectacles, do the ruins begin to speak for themselves. The Welsh ruins help to mark out the route of Giraldus Cambrensis with the archbishop round Wales. Perhaps indeed it was because he was dealing with Welshmen rather than familiar historical English figures that the ruins take on a new dimension. Hoare was already, with the help of Carter, grasping the rudiments of Gothic architecture. The building has to be at least roughly dated before you can associate it confidently with any historical person; it was the beginning, by using the material remains as the record, of what we may call archaeology.

The importance of Ruskin and Morris has been discussed. I am not too sure about 'sermons in stone'; it was the emphasis on the authentic record that the stone represented that altered the whole approach to both ruins and intact buildings. Authentic or false, for Horace Walpole it did not matter: all was material for mockery. The genuine Norman sculpture could be suspended on Shobdon Hill like an object of ridicule.[5] For the later Victorian restorer his own piety allowed original and restoration to blend together for the greater glory of God. Against this Ruskin revolted and, through Morris and the SPAB, the sacred nature of the authentic prevailed. At the same time Willis, a professor of engineering, could lay down the basis for the study of Gothic architecture.

Lubbock and Pitt-Rivers were a diversion but a very valuable one. They had no interest in 'restoration' since the prehistoric monuments spoke for themselves of the great discovery of the antiquity of man. A new technique to advance its study in the form of excavation was demonstrated by the new Inspector of Ancient Monuments in Cranborne Chase.

Lord Curzon had demonstrated in India how to create an organisation to preserve ancient monuments. On his return he demonstrated just what should be done and, in Parliament, hustled the First Commissioner of Works into legislation. The accumulation of ruins in the care of the Office of Works meant that Sir Charles Peers, working in an 'arts and crafts' atmosphere, laid down the time-honoured treatment of ruins in this country, 'treat as found'.

* * * * *

There has been a revulsion against Peers recently[6] and he has been blamed for the ugly appearance of the ruins treated in this manner. Naked ruins are inevitably ugly: they were beautiful to pursuers of the Picturesque because they were clothed in vegetation. Fountains Abbey in Yorkshire or Machu Picchu owe their famed beauty to their surroundings, artificial or natural as the case may be. Fountains or Rievaulx Abbeys planted in a flat sand desert would be most unattractive. Exposure of the low remains is universal in, for example, Classical cities of the Mediterranean area. Leptis Magna or even Pompeii shock one because of the ugliness of the remains. The truncated remains of buildings even before full construction when being built are fairly repulsive. Attempts by Evans at the palaces in Knossos or the Italians in Libya to restore rarely arouse admiration. How else can one expose what survives? Usually critics can offer no serious alternative apart from the dubious use of restoration. At least what survives is real evidence, not what Viollet-le-Duc thought ought to have been there. There is a place for creative restoration as he and Burges demonstrated but, for normal monuments without gifted architects, it is best to retain the genuine article. As with a manuscript, tinkering with the original can cause distress to those that follow.

Notes

1 Bradley 2002.
2 Quoted in Thompson 1981, 13, with reference to the Exeter Book from where it comes.
3 Peers 1931, and of course Davies 1913.
4 Waldron 1990. If indeed nearly all the visible wall is Ming (AD 1366–1644) then the Great Wall in its visible form is some 1200 years younger than Hadrian's Wall in England. This and its great bulk would account for it being so much better preserved where it survives at all. In the case of Hadrian's Wall the true original height is not known.
5 Described in Pevsner, *Herefordshire* (Buildings of England) 1963, 288–289.
6 Emerick 1998; Evans, 2004.

Appendix 1

Viollet-le-Duc on Restoration

This is a shortened version of E. Viollet-le-Duc's article *Restauration* in Volume 8, 14–24 of the *Dictionnaire raisonné de l'architecture française du XIe au XVIe siècle (1875 reprint)* The text makes clear that it was written in about 1865.

Restoration. n.f. The word and the thing are modern. To restore a building is not to maintain, repair or even remake it: it is to re-establish it in a complete state which can never have existed at any given moment.

It is only in the second quarter of our century that one has claimed to restore buildings of another age and we did not know how precisely to define architectonic restoration. Perhaps it is appropriate to give an exact account of what is understood or what one ought to understand by 'a restoration' for it seems that numerous errors have slipped into the meaning that one attaches or ought to attach to this operation.

We have said that the word and the thing are modern and in fact no civilisation, no people, in past times knew how to make restorations as we understand them today.

In Asia formerly as today when a temple or palace suffered the degradations of time another would be built or another would be erected beside it: it was abandoned to the passage of time as if that was what it belonged to. The Romans rehabilitated but did not restore, so Latin has no word corresponding to our word 'restoration', as it is understood today…To raise a triumphal arch like that of Constantine at Rome with fragments torn from the arch of Trajan is not a restoration nor a reconstruction : it is an act of vandalism, the looting of barbarians …The Empire began to restore temples at the very moment when the church was going to be substituted for them and with us there was a kind of hurry with which a number of Catholic churches were repaired and completed on the eve of the Reformation.

But the Middle Ages, no more than Antiquity, had no feeling for restorations as we understand them today, far from it. If in a building in the twelfth century a broken capital needed replacing it was a capital of the thirteenth, fourteenth or of the fifteenth century that was put in its place…

One could say that there is as much danger in restoring in facsimile what was found in an old building as in claiming to substitute for the later forms what must have existed there originally. In the first case real faith, the sincerity of the professional can produce the gravest errors in blessing, so to speak, a later interpolation: in the second the replacement of the existing form, evidently later, by the first form could remove traces of a repair of which the known cause perhaps could have permitted the occurrence of an exceptional event to be recognised…

Our age and our age only, since the beginning of historical time, has faced the past in an unusual way. It has sought to analyse, compare, classify and create its true history, pursuing step by step the course, the progress, the transformations of humanity. A fact so strange cannot be, as some superficial minds suppose, a fashion, a caprice, a sickness, for the phenomenon is too complex. Cuvier by his works on comparative anatomy, by his geological researches reveals in an instant to the eyes of his contemporaries the history of the world before it was ruled by man. The imagination eagerly follows this new road. Philologists since then discovered the origins of European languages, all derived from the same source…Finally come the archaeologists who from India up to Egypt and Europe compare, discuss, divide the artefacts revealing their origins, their affiliations and arrive, little by little, by the analytical method to pull them together following certain laws. To see fantasy and fashion in this is to weigh a little lightly a matter of some gravity. One might as well claim that the facts revealed by science, since Newton, are merely the caprice of the human mind…If the European has reached this phase of the human mind, proceeding with redoubled pace towards his future destiny, and perhaps because he moves so fast he feels the need to recover all his past, just as one assembles a large library to prepare for future work, is it reasonable to accuse him of allowing himself to be distracted by a caprice, an ephemeral fantasy?…To break down prejudice uncover forgotten truths is not this on the contrary one of the most active ways of developing progress…?

All the same these observers of the past, these archaeologists, patiently uncovering the least traces of the past that one supposed were lost have to overcome prejudices…The twelfth century in the West was a veritable renaissance, politically, socially, philosophically of art and of literature aided by men who were studying the past. The sixteenth century presents the same phenomenon. Archaeologists have no need to worry about that time of arrest that one claims to impose on them, for not only in France, but throughout Europe their work is appreciated by a public avid with them to penetrate into the very heart of previous ages…

You will ask perhaps what connections these disputes can have with the article's title: we are going to tell you this. Architects in France did not rush in. Already towards the end of the first quarter of this century literary work on the Middle Ages led to serious study so that architects did not see Gothic vaults as merely the forest of Germany (it was an hallowed phrase) and in the pointed arch just a sick art form…The churches of the Middle Ages, devastated during the Revolution, abandoned, blackened by the weather, weakened by humidity had the appearance merely of empty coffins…These witnesses of the piety (some would say fanaticism) of our fathers reflected only a half mystic and half barbarous state in which caprice ruled as master…The survey of them as monuments was avoided, attributed to the Goths as some serious persons called them. It was then that men, in no way professionals and outside the area of academic sway started a campaign with major works, remarkable for the time when they were accomplished.

In 1830 M Vitet was appointed Inspector General of Historic Monuments. This discerning scholar knew how to bring to his duties not just great archaeological knowledge that no one else could possess but a critical mind and analysis, which at once shed light exposing the history of our ancient monuments. In 1831 M Vitet addressed to the Minister of the Interior a Report, lucid and methodical, on the inspection he had just carried out of the northern departments, which revealed at once to discerning people the treasures hitherto ignored…a report that is today considered a chef d'oeuvre in this type of study. We beg permission to quote a few extracts:

> I know, says the author, that in the eyes of many people in authority it is a singular paradox to speak seriously of the sculpture of the Middle Ages. To those who believe that from the Antonines to Francis 1 there has been no question of sculpture in Europe when the statues are the work of uncouth and unskilled masons. One only needs eyes and a little faith to do justice to such prejudices…a beautiful school of sculpture, heir to and proceeding from and even in the style of Classical art…
>
> …To reconstruct or rather re-create the whole ensemble and its lesser details of a fortress of the Middle Ages, to reproduce its internal decoration and even its furniture;

in a word to create its shape, colour and I dare say its original life that is the project that has come to me straight away on entering the castle of Coucy. These immense towers, that colossal keep, seem in some respects to have been built yesterday...

Up to now this type of work has been applied only to Classical monuments. I believe that in the medieval domain it would have an even more useful result...

This programme so vividly traced by this illustrious critic 34 years ago we see realised today, not on paper, not vanishing plans, but in stone, in wood and in iron in a no-less interesting castle, that at Pierrefonds. M Vitet is the first to have turned his attention to the serious restoration of monuments, the first to have put forward practical ideas on this subject, the first to criticise the methods of work. The way was opened for other critics, for other scholars to throw themselves into it and after them the craftsmen.

At the wish of Napoleon I who was in advance of his times in all matters and who understood the importance of restoration, the church of St Denis was to serve as a mausoleum of the new dynasty as well as a sort of specimen of the progress of art from thirteenth and fourteenth centuries in France. Funds were made available for its restoration... The unhappy church of St Denis was like a corpse upon which the first craftsmen pursuing restoration practised.

It is now time to explain the programme followed today in England and Germany that we had reached in the course of our theoretical studies of the former arts, accepted in Italy and Spain in their turn to introduce a critical approach into the conservation of their ancient monuments.

This programme allows straightaway that in principle a building must be restored in the style to which it belongs not only in appearance but also in its structure. There are few buildings, particularly in the Middle Ages, that have been erected at one go, or if they have, have not experienced major modifications either by additions, transformations or necessary changes. It is essential before any repair work to establish the age and character of each part in order to set out a report form based on precise notes either written or drawings. For in France each province has its own individual style, which must be known with its principles and methods. The data for a monument in the Ile de France cannot serve to restore a building in Champagne or Burgundy. These differences of schools persist very late....

But for those dealing with the Middle Ages there are accumulating difficulties facing restorers. Often the monuments or parts of monuments of one period and school have been replaced at different times and done by craftsmen who did not belong to the province where the building was erected. Hence much embarrassment. If it is a question of restoring the original parts as well as the altered parts must one take account of this and re-establish the unity of the altered parts? So the absolute adoption of either of these two divisions is dangerous, and it is necessary on the contrary not to bind oneself absolutely but to do as the particular circumstances may require...Above all, before being an archaeologist, the architect in charge must be a skilled and experienced builder...he must know the procedures used in construction at different periods of our art and of various schools. It is not a matter here, as in the previous case of preserving an improvement in a defective system, but considering that the later restoration has been made uncritically, following methods applied to the present day, which consisted in all restitution or restoration of adopting the system in use at the time: we work on the opposite principle of restoring every building in the style appropriate to it. But these vaults, foreign to the earlier ones which one reconstructs, are remarkably beautiful and are associated with large windows with painted glass and a system of external buttressing of great value. Would one destroy all this to have the satisfaction of the original nave in its purity?...No certainly. It can be seen that absolute principles in these matters can lead to absurdity...

There exist certain cathedrals in France among those rebuilt at the end of the twelfth century, which had no kind of transepts. In the fourteenth and fifteenth centuries transepts have been added on two or three bays. These modifications have been more or less skilfully done, but to the practiced eye traces of the original have been left. In these cases the restorer must be over-meticulous and must emphasise the traces of the modifications that have been made…

If the architect responsible for restoration of a building must know the forms, the styles belonging to it and the schools from which they derive it is better still, if possible to know its structure, its anatomy, its temperament for above all he has to make it live. He should penetrate into every part of the structure, as if he himself had erected it, and this knowledge requires he must have ready several ways of doing the work of reclamation. If one method fails a second and a third must be ready to hand.

Let us not forget that monuments of the Middle Ages are not constructed like monuments of the Roman age of which the structure operates by passive resistance opposed to active forces. In the structures of the Middle Ages every member plays its part. If the vault pushes, the buttress or flying buttress counters the thrust. If a springer breaks it is not sufficient to give vertical support one must counter the various forces that act on it in the opposite direction. If an arch is distorted it is not sufficient to put up centring for it abuts other arches which have an oblique action…It is a war, a series of exercises which have to be modified each day from ceaseless observation of the effects being produced…

These are the factors with which the experienced architects juggles but always having ten methods to prevent an accident in such a way that he inspires sufficient confidence in his workmen so that panic does not remove the means to cope with any situation without delay, without fumbling and without showing fear…

Works of restoration, which from a serious practical point of view belong to our time, bring honour with them. They have forced architects to extend their knowledge and acquire resourceful, expeditious methods of work; to put themselves into closer association with building workers, to teach them, and to form centres either in the provinces or Paris which allow the best qualified craftsmen of all to enter the great workshops.

It is thanks to the restoration works that important industries have arisen, that the working of masonry has become more skilled, that the use of materials has become widespread; for architects in charge of restoration in obscure villages lacking everything have exploited quarries by opening old ones. The administrative centralisation of France has its merits and advantages, which we do not query: it has consolidated political unity but we must not conceal its inconveniences. Speaking only of architectural centralisation it has taken not only the stylistic schools from the provinces and with them the particular methods, skills, local industries…The school of architecture established at Paris, and at Paris only, had other ambitions; it created laureates for the Academy of France, good architects but little suited to the run of work in France in the nineteenth century. Certainly the first who thought of saving from ruin the most beautiful buildings on our soil bequeathed from the past and who organised the service of historic monuments, acted only under the influence of professionals. They were frightened at the destruction threatening all such remarkable remains and the acts of vandalism carried out each day with the blandest indifference…

The work of restoration undertaken in France at first under the *Commission des monuments historiques,* and later the building services of *Diocesains* have not only saved from ruin works of undisputed value but have provided a service of immediate response. The work of the Commission has thus to a certain point combatted the dangers of administrative centralisation in public works; it has achieved for the provinces what the *Ecole des Beaux Arts* did not know how to give…

But it is in the circumstances that often arise that the architect must exercise his wisdom. He has always to reconcile his role as restorer with that of a professional responsible for meeting unforeseen needs. Furthermore the best means of preserving a building is to find a use for it and to meet all the requirements that this may require. For example it is clear that the responsible architect engaged on the beautiful refectory of St Martin des Champs to convert it into a library for the *Ecole des arts et metiers* had to take account, while respecting and restoring the building to organise the rack compartments in such a way that there never arose a need to return and alter the lay-out of the hall…

That an architect refuses to allow gas pipes into a church in order to avoid mutilation and accidents is understandable because the building can be lit by other means but the provision of a stove, for example, is denied under the pretext that the Middle Ages did not adopt this form of heating in religious buildings, which causes the worshippers to catch cold for the sake of archaeology, this has become ridiculous…In a medieval structure every part of the whole fulfils a function and has a purpose. It is to the knowing exactly the value of the one and the other that the architect must devote himself before embarking on anything. He must imitate a skilled and experienced surgeon who touches an organ only after having a full knowledge of its function and having foreseen the immediate and further consequences of his operation. If it is a question of luck it were better he abstained. Better to let the patient die than to kill him…

But photography presents this advantage of constituting an undeniable record that one can study at all times even when the restoration conceals traces left on the ruin. Photography has naturally led architects to be even more scrupulous in their respect for the least traces of former arrangements…

There is in making a restoration a dominant principle which one must never under any pretext whatsoever ignore: that is to take account of all evidence revealing a lay-out… Also when it is a matter of completing a building that is partly ruined before starting it is necessary to thoroughly excavate the ground, examine everything, join the smallest pieces together taking care to establish where they were found…

We have said enough to allow us to grasp the difficulties to be taken account of by an architect undertaking restoration if he takes his duties seriously and if he wishes not only to appear sincere but not having on his conscience anything left to chance nor of ever being consciously mistaken.

Appendix 2

Darwin and Lubbock

Lubbock enjoyed a close friendship with Charles Darwin up to the latter's death in 1882, even acting as a pall-bearer at his funeral in Westminster Abbey. The publication of Darwin's *Correspondence*, at the time of writing (2005) now up to 1865 (volume 13), by Cambridge University Press, has thrown much light on the relationship during Lubbock's formative years.

The Lubbocks were already established at Down when Darwin moved into an adjoining property in January 1846, taking a lease from Sir J. W. Lubbock, the father of Lubbock, of adjoining land to extend his 'walks'. Sir J. W. Lubbock was a distinguished physicist, former Treasurer and Vice President of the Royal Society *(DNB)*.

Lubbock junior was a child when Darwin became his neighbour and we first hear of him as a boy of about 14 when Darwin arranged the purchase of a microscope for his father to give Lubbock (*Correspondence,* vol. 4, p.184). This was about the time Lubbock abandoned Classical studies at Eton and started to teach himself biology. In 1851, when he was 17, Darwin referred to 'John Lubbock, the eldest son of Sir John, my neighbour, who has taken a passion for dissecting...' (*Correspondence,* vol. 5, p.52). In the same volume Darwin sent beetles to Lubbock (p.281) and thanked him for his leipidoptera books (p.378).

There are other references to be culled from the *Correspondence* but the most interesting is in April 1859 when Darwin had already decided that Natural Selection was the solution to Evolution when he wrote 'my neighbour and excellent naturalist is an enthusiastic convert' (*Correspondence,* vol. 7 p. 279). Lubbock was involved with evolution even when Darwin was still working out its explanation.

When Lubbock was contemplating moving to Brighton in August 1861 Darwin wrote to him 'how much I enjoyed your friendship and what a loss your absence will be to me' (*Correspondence,* vol. 9, p. 235). Lubbock only moved to Chislehurst and later moved back to Down.

Lubbock was an accomplished and respected biologist when he took up 'prehistory', already a Fellow of the Royal Society. Darwin was full of praise for the style of *Prehistoric Times*: 'The latter half of your book has been read out aloud to me and the style is so clever and easy (we both think it perfection) that I am beginning at the beginning...' (*Correspondence,* vol. 13, p. 182). As Lubbock said some years later: 'the methods of archaeological investigation are as trustworthy as those of any natural science' (Lubbock, 1879, 139). His whole approach to the past was moulded by his biological background.

Appendix 3

The Schedule to the 1882 Act

The Ancient Monuments Protection Act of 1882 had a Schedule attached of 'monuments to which it applies' where Pitt-Rivers had to persuade the owners to put them into 'guardianship'. It is very similar but not identical to the Schedule of Lubbock's Bill which had failed in 1880. Note that English monuments were almost exclusively prehistoric but Scotland and Ireland had a sprinkling of early medieval monuments in their lists. Except for brochs, masonry appears absent from the monuments in the list.

The Schedule
List of monuments to which this Act applies

England and Wales

	County	Parish
The tumulus and dolmen, Plas Newydd	Anglesea	Llandedwen
The tumulus known as Wyland Smith's Forge	Berkshire	Ashbury
Uffington Castle	Berkshire	Uffington
The stone circle known as Long Meg and her Daughters, near Penrith	Cumberland	Addingham
The stone circle on Castle Rigg, near Keswick	Cumberland	Crosthwaite
The stone circles on Burn Moor	Derbyshire	St Bees
The stone circle known as The Nine Ladies, Stanton Moor	Derbyshire	Bakewell
The tumulus known as Arbor Low	Derbyshire	Bakewell
Hob Hurst's House and Hut, Bastow Moor	Derbyshire	Bakewell
Minning Low	Derbyshire	Brassington
Arthur's Quoit, Gower	Glamorganshire	Llanridian
The tumulus at Uley	Gloucestershire	Uley
Kit's Coty House	Kent	Aylesford
Danes Camp	Northamptonshire	Hardingstone
Castle Dykes	Northamptonshire	Farthinstone
The Rollrich Stones	Oxfordshire	Little Rollright
Pentre Evan Cromlech	Pembrokeshire	Nevern
The ancient stones at Stanton Drew	Somersetshire	Stanton Drew
The chambered tumulus at Stoney Littleton, Wellow	Somersetshire	Wellow
Cadbury Castle	Somersetshire	South Cadbury
Mayborough, near Penrith	Westmorland	Barton

	County	Parish
Arthur's Round Table	Westmorland	Barton
The group of stones known as Stonehenge	Wiltshire	Amesbury
Old Sarum	Wiltshire	Amesbury
The vallum at Abury, the Sarcen stones within the same, those along Kennet Road and the group between Abury and Beckhampton	Wiltshire	Abury
The long barrow at West Kennet, near Marlborough	Wiltshire	West Kennet
Silbury Hill	Wiltshire	Abury
The dolmen (Devil's Den), near Marlborough	Wiltshire	Fyfield
Barbury Castle	Wiltshire	Ogbourne, St. Andrews, and Swindon

Scotland

	County	Parish
The Bass of Inverury	Aberdeenshire	Inverurie
The vitrified fort on the hill of Noath	Aberdeenshire	Rhynie
The pillar and stone at Newton in-the-Garioch	Aberdeenshire	Culsalmond
The circular walled structures called 'Edin's Hall' on Cockburn Law	Berwickshire	Dunse
The British walled settlement enclosing huts at Harefaulds in Lauderdale	Berwickshire	Lauder
The Dun of Dorndilla	Sutherlandshire	Durness
The sculptured stone called Suenos Stone, near Forres	Elgin	Rafford
The cross slab, with inscription, in the churchyard of St Vigeans	Forfarshire	St Vigeans
The British forts, on the hills, called The Black & White Catherthuns	Forfarshire	Menmuir
A group of remains and pillars, on a haugh at Clava on the banks of the Nairn	Inverness	Croy and Dalecross
The Pictish towers at Glenelg	Inverness	Glenelg
The cairns, with chambers and galleries partially dilapidated	Kirkcudbrightshire	Minigaff
The Catstane, an inscribed pillar	Linlithgow	Kirkliston
The Ring of Brogar and other stone pillars at Stennis in Orkney, and the neighbouring pillars	Orkney	Firth & Stennis
The chambered mound of Maeshowe	Orkney	Firth and Stennis
The stones of Callernish	Ross	Uig
The Burgh of Clickanim	Shetland	Sound
The Pictish tower at Mousa in Shetland	Shetland	Dunrossness
The inscribed slab standing to the road leading from Wigton to Whithorn and about a mile from Whithorn	Wigtonshire	Whithorn
Two stones with incised crosses on a mound in a field at Laggangairn	Wigtonshire	New Luce
The pillars at Kirkmadrine	Wigtonshire	Stoneykirk

Ireland

			(Barony)
The earthen enclosure & mounds called the Navan Fort	Armagh	Eglish	Armagh
Stone monuments & groups of sepulchral cists in Glen Maulin	Donegal	Glencolumbkille	Banagh
The earthen & stone inclosure known as Grianan of Aileach	Donegal	Burt	West Innisowen
The earthen inclosure & Cromlech called Giant's Ring near Ballylessan	Down	Drumbo	Upper Castlereagh
The earthen fort of Downpatrick (Dunkeltair)	Down	Downpatrick	Lecale
Stone structure called Staigue Fort	Kerry	Kilcrogham	Dunkerron
The earthen mound at Greenmount	Kerry	Kilsaran	Ardee
The stone monument at Ballyna	Mayo	Kilmoremoy	Tyrawly
Cairns & stone circles at Moytura	Mayo	Cong	Kilmaine
The tumuli, New Grange, Knowth & Dowth	Meath	Monknewton	Upper Slane & Dowth
The earthworks on the hill of Tara	Meath	Tara	Skreen
The earthworks at Teltown (Taltin)	Meath	Teltown	Upper Skells
The earthworks at Wardstown (Tlaghta)	Meath	Athboy	Lune
The two central tumuli on the hills called Slieve Na Calliagh	Meath	Longhcrew	Fore
The cairn at Heapstown	Sligo	Kilmacallan	Tirerrill
Sepulchral remains at Carrowmore	Sligo	Kilmacowen	Curbury
The cairn called Miscaw Mave or Knocknarea			
The cave containing Ogham inscribed stones at Drumlogham	Waterford	Stradbally	Decies without Drum
The stone monument called the Catstane and the cemetery on the hill of Usnagh	Westmeath	Killare	Rathconrath

Appendix 4

List of Relevant Acts

Asterisk means the Act has since been repealed

1869   *Irish Church Act*. At disestablishment, ecclesiastical ruins 'vested' in Irish Board of Works under Superintendent, later Inspector.

1882   *Ancient Monuments Protection Act*. Emasculated form of Lubbock's Bill that had failed in 1880. Predominantly prehistoric monuments, megalithic or earthworks in Schedule at end. Created Inspector. 'Permissive'.

1900   *Ancient Monuments Protection Act*. Amendments to 1882 Act.

1910   *Ancient Monuments Protection Act*. County Councils to take on monuments and redefining 'monument' to include masonry structures.

1913   *Ancient Monuments Consolidation and Amendment Act*. Introduction of degree of compulsion. Created Advisory Boards for England, Scotland and Wales.

1931   *Ancient Monuments Act*. Increased penalties for damage including up to three months' imprisonment. Refined scheduling process.

1953   *Historic Buildings and Ancient Monuments Act*. Created Historic Buildings Councils but much of it repealed.

1979   *Archaeology Areas Act*. Swept away earlier legislation including 1913 Act, statutory inspectors etc. Archaeology Areas were recognition of the central part now played by excavation. Reformed the executive side of work.

1983   *National Heritage Act*. Took ancient monuments and other bodies out of Government. Created Historic Buildings and Ancient Monuments Commission, usually called English Heritage, combining the two functions in one body. Not covering Wales or Scotland. Much in keeping with period.

Appendix 5

Ruined Monasteries and Castles in State Care in 1970s in England and Wales

These lists have been extracted from the published *List of Ancient Monuments in England corrected to 31ˢᵗ December 1971 (HMSO) and List of Monuments in Wales corrected to 31ˢᵗ December, 1974 (HMSO)*. Most remains will have received some treatment of masonry. The abbreviations are for pre-1974 county names; A, abbey; P, priory; F, friary and C, castle. Often only a part in care, e.g. merely a gatehouse.

Monasteries:

Abbotsbury. A, Dor.
Basingwerk A, Flint.
Binham P, Norf.
Brinkburn P, Northumb.
Buildwas A, Shrop.
Bury St Edmunds A, Suff.
Byland A, Yorks.
Canterbury, St Augustine's A, Kent
Castle Acre P, Norf.
Cleeve A, Som.
Colchester, St Botolphs P, Essex
Creake A, Norf.
Colchester, St John's Abbey gatehouse, Essex
Creak A, Norf.
Croxden A, Staffs.
Cymmer A, Merion.
Denbigh F, Den.
Denny A, Cambs.
Easby A, Yorks.
Egglestone A, Yorks.
Ewenny P, Glam.
Finchale P, Dur.
Fountains A, Yorks.
Furness A, Lancs.
Gisborough P, Yorks.
Gloucester A, gatehouse
Gloucester F, Blackfriars
Great Yarmouth, Greyfriars cloister, Norf.

Hailes A, Glos.
Haughmond A, Shrop.
Isleham P, Cambs.
Jarrow P, Dur.
Kingswood A, Glos.
Kirkham P, Yorks.
Lanercrost P, Cumb.
Leiston A, Suff.
Lilleshall P, Shrop.
Lindisfarne P, Northumb.
Llanthony P, Mon.
Malling A, Kent
Mattersey A, Notts.
Monk Bretton P, Yorks.
Mount Grace P, Yorks.
Muchelney A, Som.
Neath A, Glam.
Netley A, Hants.
North Creake A, Norf.
Penmon P, Anglesey
Richmond, Greyfriars tower, Yorks.
Rievaulx A, Yorks.
Roche A, Yorks.
Rufford A, Notts.
Ryland A, Yorks.
St Dogmael's A, Pemb.
St Olave's P, Suff.
Sawley A, Yorks. (now Lancs.)
Sempringham P, Lincs.
Shap A, Cumb.
Southwick P, Hants.
Stamford, Whitefriars gate,

Lincs.
Strata Florida A, Flint.
Talley A, Carm.
Thetford P (Cluniac), Norf.
Thornton A, Lincs.
Tintagel A, Corn.
Tintern A, Mon.
Titchfield A, Hants.
Tynemouth P, Northumb.
Valle Crucis A, Denb.
Venlock A, Shrop.
Whitby A, Yorks.

Castles:

Acton Burnell C, Shrop.
Ashby de la Zouche C, Leics.
Aydon C, Northumb.
Baconsthorpe C, Norf.
Barnard C, Dur.
Beaumaris C, Anglesey
Beeston C, Ches.
Bearscore C, Dev.
Berkhamsted C, Herts.
Berwick upon Tweed C, Northumb.
Bolingbroke C, Lincs.
Bolsover C, Derby.
Bolton C, Yorks.
Bowes C, Yorks.
Bronllys C, Breck.
Caernarfon C, Caer.
Caerphilly C, Glam.

Camber C, Sur.
Carlisle C, Cumb.
Carreg Cennen C, Carm.
Castell Coch, Glam.
Castell y Bere, Merion.
Castle Acre C, Norf.
Castle Rising, Norf.
Chepstow C, Mon.
Chester C, Ches.
Cilgerran C, Pemb.
Clifford's Tower, Yorks.
Coity C, Glam.
Conisborough C, Yorks.
Conwy C, Caer.
Cromwell's C, Scilly
Dartmouth C, Dev.
Deal C, Kent
Deddington C, Oxon.
Denbigh C, Denb.
Dolbadarn C, Caer.
Dolforwyn C, Mont.
Dolwyddelan C, Caer.
Donnington C, Berks.
Dover C, Kent
Dunstanburgh C, Northumb.
Ewloe C, Flint.
Eynesford C, Kent
Farleigh C, Som.
Farnham C, Sur.
Fort Brockhurst, Hants.

Framlingham C, Suff.
Goodrich C, Heref.
Grosmont C, Mon.
Hadleigh C, Essex
Harlech C, Merion.
Harry's Walls, Scilly
Helmsley C, Yorks.
Hurst C, Hants.
Hylton C, Dur.
Kenilworth C, Warw.
Kidwelly C, Carm.
King Charles C, Scilly
Kirby C, Leics.
Laugharne C, Carm.
Launceston C, Corn.
Llanstephan C, Carm.
Llawhaden C, Pemb.
Longtown C, Heref.
Loughor C, Glam.
Ludgershall C, Wilts.
Middleham C, Yorks.
Monmouth C, Mon.
Montgomery C, Mont.
Moreton Corbet C, Shrop.
Newcastle C, Glam.
Newport C, Mon.
Norham C, Northumb.
Nunney C, Som.
Ogmore C, Glam.
Oldblockhouse, Scilly

Orford C, Suff.
Oxwich C, Glam.
Pendennis, C, Corn.
Penrith C, Cumb.
Pevensey C, Kent
Peveril C, Derb.
Pickering C, Yorks.
Portland C, Dor.
Prudhoe C, Northumb.
Raglan C, Mon.
Restormel c, Corn.
Rhuddlan C, Flint.
Richmond C, Yorks.
St Catharine's C, Corn.
St Mawes C, Corn.
Scarborough C, Yorks.
Sherborne C, Dor.
Skenfrith C, Mon.
Skipsea C, Yorks.
Spofforth C, Yorks.
Swansea C, Glam.
Tilbury Fort, Essex
Tintagel C, Corn.
Totnes C, Devon
Tretower C, Breck.
Tynemouth C, Northumb.
Weeting C, Norf.
Wobley C, Glam.
White C, Mon.

Appendix 6

International Charter on Preservation of Monuments, Venice, 1964

The International Congress for Architects and Technicians of Historic Monuments held at Venice in May 1964 produced an *International Charter on the Preservation and Restoration of Cultural Monuments and Monuments' Areas*. Its text appears to be unavailable in this country but a German version was published in *Osterreichische Zeitschrift fur Kunst und Denkmal Pflege 22* (1968) 100–101, and I have accordingly translated the relevant parts, that is Articles 9–14 below:

Restoration

Article 9 – Restoration always has the character of an exceptional step to preserve and show aesthetic and historic value. It is based on respect for the original structure and authentic sources. It is restricted to the point where hypothesis begins: that is where hypothetical reconstruction is in question to complete the structure that on aesthetic and technical grounds was unavoidably necessary to round off an architectonic composition and show it in the character of our time. Before treatment and during restoration investigations will be carried out continually.

Article 10 – If traditional methods appear inadequate then the restoration of a monument can be secured by employing all modern conservation expertise and procedures of which the effectiveness through scientific knowledge and practical experience has been guaranteed.

Article 11 – The contributions from every period to the building must be respected. Style purity is in no sense among the objectives in a restoration. If a structure shows a sequence of different builds the uncovering of earlier stages is only exceptionally justified if the removed elements are of minor significance, and the uncovered masonry represents evidence of overriding historical, scientific or aesthetic value and the project itself is sufficiently important. A judgement on the value of the elements in question and the decision on the parts being removed cannot be taken alone by the person himself undertaking the work.

Article 12 – The elements which have been chosen to replace missing parts must be in sympathetic blend but quite divorced from the original so that the value of the monument as a historical document is not falsified.

Article 13 – Alterations can only be made so long as all the original structural members of a monument, its traditional framework, the harmony of its composition and its relationship to its surroundings are respected.

The Monument Area

Article 14 – The monument area must be subject to special care so that its integrity, functional renewal of its adaptation and new life can be assured. The preservation and restoration works are so conducted that they represent a sensible application of the basic principles of the preceding articles.

Bibliography

Andrews, J H 1975. *A Paper Landscape: the Ordnance Survey in nineteenth-century Ireland*, Oxford

Anon, 1903. *Notes on the Repair of Ancient Buildings*, SPAB, London

Ashbee, C R 1901. *An Endeavour towards the Teaching of John Ruskin and William Morris*, London

Batchelor, J 2000. *John Ruskin: no wealth but life*, London

Bowden, M 1991. *Pitt-Rivers, the life and archaeological work of Lieutenant-General Augustus Henry Lane Fox Pitt Rivers, DCL, FRS, FSA*, Cambridge

Briggs, M S 1952. *Goths and Vandals: A study of the destruction, neglect and preservation of historical buildings in England*, London

Bradley, R 2002. *The Past in Prehistoric Societies*, London

Britton, J 1807–26. *The architectural antiquities of Great Britain: represented and illustrated in a series of views, elevations, plans, sections and details of various ancient edifices: with historical and descriptive accounts of each*, 5 vols

Brooks, M 1987. *John Ruskin and Victorian Architecture*, London

Brown, G B 1905. *The Care of Ancient Monuments*, London

Burkhardt, F and Matt, S (eds) 1985 in progress. *The Correspondence of Charles Darwin*, 13 vols, Cambridge

Butler, L 1989. 'Dolforwyn Castle, Monygomery, Powys. First report: the excavations 1981–1986', *Archaeol Cambrensis*, **138**, 78–98

Butler, L 1995. 'Dolforwyn Castle, Monygomery, Powys. Second report: the excavations 1987–1990', *Archaeol Cambrensis*, **144**, 133–203

Cantacuzion, S (ed) 1975. *Architectural Conservation in Europe*, London

Chippendale, C 1983. 'The making of the first Ancient Monuments Act, 1882, and its administration under General Pitt Rivers', *J. British Archaeol. Assoc.* **136**, 1–55

Choay, F 2000. (English translation). *The invention of the historic monument*, New York

Colvin, Sir Howard (ed) 1963–82. *History of the King's Works*, 6 vols, London

Coppack, G and Gilyard-Beer, R 1986. 'Excavation at Fountains Abbey, North Yorkshire 1979–80: the early development of the monastery', *Archaeologia*, **108**, 147–87

Coxe, W 1801. *An Historical Tour of Monmouthshire; illustrated with views by Sir R. C. Hoare, Bart., a new map of the county, and other engravings*, 2 vols, London

Curzon, G N 1892. *Persia and the Persian Question*, London

Curzon, G N 1906. *Lord Curzon in India, being a selection from his speeches as Viceroy and Governor General of India, 1898–1905. With a portrait, explanatory notes, and an index, and with an introduction by Sir Thomas Raleigh*, London

Curzon, G N 1926. *Bodiam Castle, Sussex. A historical and descriptive survey*, London

Curzon, Marquis G N and Tipping, H A 1929. *Tattershall Castle, Lincolnshire. A historical and descriptive survey*, London

Daniel, G E 1950. *A Hundred Years of Archaeology*, London

Davies, W J 1913. 'The Preservation of Ancient Monuments', *J Roy Inst Brit Architect*, **20**, 533–52, 594–608

Duff, U G (ed) 1934. *The Lifework of Lord Avebury*, London

Edwardes, M 1965. *High Noon of Empire: India under Curzon*, London

Emerick, K 1998. 'Sir Charles Peers and After: from frozen monuments to fluid landscapes', in Arnold, J

Davies, K and Ditchfield, S (eds) *History and heritage: consuming the past in contemporary culture*, Shaftesbury, 183–95

Emmerson, Sir Harold 1956. *The Ministry of Works*, London

Evans, D M 2004. 'Et in Arcadia? The Problems with Ruins', *Antiq J*, **84**, 411–20

Fedden, R 1968. *The continuing purpose: a history of the National Trust, its aims and work*, London

Fenton, R 1811. *A historic tour through Pembrokeshire*, London

Garrigan, K O 1973. *Ruskin on architecture: his thought and influence*, Madison

Gilmour, D 1994. *Curzon: imperial statesman 1859–1925*, London

Hardy, T 1906. 'Memories of Church restoration', *Report of SPAB*, **29**, 59–80

Harris, J 1963. 'The Ruskin Gold Medal Controversy', *J Roy Inst Brit Architect*, **70**, 165–7

Hoare, Sir Richard Colt 1806. *The Itinerary of Archbishop Baldwin through Wales AD 1188, translated into English, and illustrated with views, annotations and a life of Giraldus*, 2 vols, London

Hoare, Sir Richard Colt 1807. *Journal of a tour in Ireland AD 1806*, London

Hoare, Sir Richard Colt 1812–1821 reprinted in 1975 with an Introduction by Simmons, J and Simpson, D D A *The ancient history of Wiltshire*, 2 vols, Wakefield

Hope, Sir W St J 1900. 'Fountains Abbey', *Yorkshire Archaeol J*, **15**, 269–400

Hope, Sir W St J 1905. 'Architectural history of Mount Grace', *Yorkshire Archaeol J*, **18** 270–310

Hutchinson, H G 1914. *Life of Sir John Lubbock, Lord Avebury*, 2 vols, London

Kains–Jackson, C P with a preface by Sir John Lubbock 1880. *Our Ancient Monuments and the Land Around them*, London

Kennet, W 1972. *Preservation*, London

Lubbock, Sir John, later Lord Avebury 1865. *Prehistoric times as illustrated by ancient remains and the manners and customs of modern savages*, London

Lubbock, Sir John, later Lord Avebury, 1868. *Nilson and the Stone Age*, London

Lubbock, Sir John, later Lord Avebury 1870. *The Origin of Civilisation and the Primitive Condition of Man*, London

Lubbock, Sir John, later Lord Avebury 1874. *Addresses, Scientific, Political and Educational*

Macaulay, R 1953. *Pleasure of Ruins*, London

MacCarthy, F 1994. *William Morris, a life for our time*, London

Morris, W 1914. *Collected papers: vol 22*, 'Hopes and Fears for Art', 'Lectures on Art and Industry' reprinted 1992

Mosley, L 1960. *Curzon, the End of an Epoch*, London

Murphy, G 1987. *Founders of the National Trust*, London

Nichols, J B 1840. *Catalogue of the Hoare Library at Stourhead, Co Wilts*, London

Owen, F 1955. *Tempestuous Journey: Lloyd George, his life and Times*, New York

Peers, Sir Charles 1931. 'Treatment of Old Buildings', *J Roy Inst Brit Architect*, **38**, 25–31

Pennant, T 1775–81. *Tours of Wales*, 3 vols, 2nd edn, 1810

Pevsner, Sir Nikolaus 1969. *Ruskin and Viollet-le-Duc: Englishness and Frenchness in the appreciation of Gothic architecture*, London

Pevsner, Sir Nikolaus 1970. *Robert Willis*, Northampton, Mass

Piggott, S 1976 'Ruins in a Landscape: Aspects of Seventeenth and Eighteenth Century Antiquarianism' and 'The Origin of the English County Archaeological Societies', in Piggott, S *Ruins in a Landscape*, Edinburgh

Pitt-Rivers, A H L F, 1887–98. *Excavations in Cranborne Chase*, 4 vols, privately printed

Pitt-Rivers, A H L F, edited by J L Myres 1906. *The Evolution of Culture and other Essays*, Oxford

Powys, A R 1929. *Repair of Ancient Buildings*, London

Prestwich, J 1859. 'On the Occurrence of Flint Implements, associated with the Remains of Extinct Mammalia in Undisturbed Beds of Late Geological Period', *Proceedings of the Royal Society of London*, **10**, 50–59

Pugh, E 1816. *Cambria Depicta: a tour through North Wales, illustrated with picturesque views … by a native artist*, London

Pugh, R B 1970. *The Victoria History of the Counties of England: General Introduction*, Oxford

Reed, F H 1872. *Illustrations of Tattershall Castle, Lincolnshire*, Sleaford

Report from H M Ambassadors at Vienna and Paris showing systems adopted in Hungary and France for Preservation of Ancient Monuments (1912), 1914, Cmd 7151

Reports of the Inspector of Ancient Monuments for 1911 (Cmd 5960), for 1912, (Cmd 6510), for 1913, (Cmd 7258)

Ronaldshay, Earl of, edited by Marquess Dundas 1928. *The life of Lord Curzon: being the authorised biography of George Nathaniel, Marquess Curzon of Kedleston*, 3 vols

Rose, K 1969. *Superior Person: a portrait of Curzon and his circle in late Victorian England*, London

Roy, W 1793. *The Military Antiquities of the Romans in North Britain*, London

Ruskin, J 1849. *The Seven Lamps of Architecture*, 1910 reprint

Ruskin, J 1854. 'The Opening of the Crystal Palace' in the *Works of John Ruskin*, vol 12, 416

Ruskin, J 1904. edited by Cook, E T and Wedderburn, A *The works of John Ruskin*, London

Saunders, A D 1983. 'A Century of Ancient Monuments Legisation', *Antiq J*, **63**, 11–24

Simpson W D 1960. *The Building Accounts of Tattershall Castle 1434–72*, Lincoln Record Society **45**

Thompson, A H 1928. *Tattershall: the Manor, the Castle, the Church*, Lincoln

Thompson, A H 1929. *A Bibliography of the Published Writings of Sir William St John Hope with a brief introductory memoir*, Leeds

Thompson, M W 1959. ' Excavation of a fortified medieval hall at Hutton Colswain at Huttons Ambo, nr Malton, Yorkshire', *Arch J*, **114**, 69–81

Thompson, M W 1960. 'The first Inspector of Ancient Monuments in the Field', *JBAA*, **23**, 103–24

Thompson, M W 1974. *Tattershall Castle, Lincolsnhire*, NT Guidebook

Thompson, M W 1977. *General Pitt-Rivers, Evolution and Archaeology in the Nineteenth Century*, Bradford on Avon

Thompson, M W 1981. *Ruins, their preservation and display*, London

Thompson, M W (ed) 1983. *The Journeys of Sir Richard Colt Hoare through Wales and England, 1793–1810 Extracted from his Journals*, Gloucester

Thompson, M W 1990. *The Cambridge Antiquarian Society, 1840–1990*, Cambridge

Thompson, M W 1996. 'Robert Willis and the Study of Medieval Architecture' in Tatton-Brown, T and Munby, J *The Archaeology of Cathedrals*, Oxford Monograph **42**

Thompson, M W and Renfrew, C 1999. 'The Catalogue of the Pitt-Rivers Museum, Farnham Dorset' *Antiquity*, **73**, 377–93

Tschudi-Madsen, S 1967. *Restoration and anti Restoration: A study in English Restoration Philosophy*, Oslo, 2nd ed

Ulbert, G and Weber, G 1985. *Konserivte Geschitchte? antike Bauten und ihre Erhaltung*, Stuttgart

Viollet-le-Duc, E 1875. (reprinted) *Dictionnaire raisonné de l'architecture française de XIme au XVIme siècles*, 10 vols, Paris

Waldron, A 1990. *The Great Wall of China*, Cambridge

Wheeler, H 1975. 'The State's Participation' in *Conservation, an Irish View'*, The Architectural Association of Ireland, Dublin, 79–94

Woodbridge, K 1970. *Landscape and Antiquity: Aspects of English culture at Stourhead, 1718–1838*, Oxford

Wyndham, H P 1775. *A Gentleman's Tour through Monmouth and Wales in the Months of June and July, 1774*, Salisbury, 2nd ed 1781

Index